Empty Collars

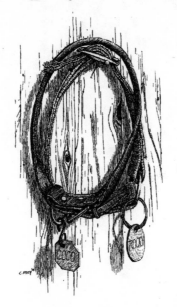

A TRIBUTE TO THE MEMORY OF OUR GUN DOGS

Empty Collars

EDITED BY
David A. Webb

GLADE RUN PRESS
GREENSBURG · PENNSYLVANIA

Illustrations copyright © 2003 by Chris Smith.
Cover and interior design: Lurelle Cheverie
Printed and bound at Versa Press, East Peoria, IL.

5 4 3 2 1

GLADE RUN PRESS
1000 Village Drive
Greensburg, Pennsylvania 15601
(724) 837-5388

ISBN: 0-9743212-0-6

Library of Congress Control Number: 2003109737

To my wife, Emma,

for her tolerance of my gun dogs.

Contents

Acknowledgments

If life were fair, our gun dogs would have the same life span as we do. But it just does not work that way. To the hunter, nothing is sadder than watching his four-legged partner struggle afield as the dog becomes older.

It is with this thought in mind that I want to express appreciation to all our gun dogs, which have given so much joy. It is for all those years in the field and their passion for the hunt. There was one particular Brittany that inspired the compilation of these stories. Her name was Magnum Magic Coco.

Several individuals provided much needed assistance with this project. Tom Pappas encouraged me many years ago to find a way to publish the book after it had been initially rejected.

Next, I would like to thank Chris Cornell for writing the Foreword and for his recommendation that I consider publishing the anthology. This has created a new adventure in publishing known as Glade Run Press.

This volume has been enhanced by the cover art and line drawings produced by the artistic talents of Chris Smith. In addition, I am grateful to the authors of the eighteen stories that are within the covers of this book. Their contribution, and granting permission to use their works, has been most appreciated.

Acknowledgments

The back inside flap of the dust jacket has a picture of my Brittany, Dewey, and the editor. We were competing in the Michigan-Saginaw field trial – first week in December 2002. I thank Bob Martin for taking this photograph.

Last, but not least, I wish to thank Melissa Hayes and Lurelle Cheverie for their creative skills in preparing the manuscript for publication. Also, I want to thank Alice Devine and Jean Ewers for their invaluable help in proofreading the book. In addition, Tom Frank has been a great help with the publication aspects of this project. Thank you all.

David Webb

CHRIS CORNELL

Foreword

CHRIS CORNELL is the editor at Countrysport Press, a Maine-based publisher of books on wingshooting, fly fishing, and gun dogs. A lifelong hunter, salt-water fisherman, and amateur gun-dog trainer, he is currently the vice-president of the Maine Retriever Trial Club, in whose events he competes with his black Lab, Star.

We all know it's coming because as longtime gun-dog owners, we have come to accept the inescapable truth that we will outlive our canine hunting partners. Yet the death of a treasured gun dog isn't an intellectual experience; it's a deeply emotional one. And we are rarely ready, no matter what the circumstances.

Yet, painful though it always is, the loss of a working dog—a teammate and friend—offers us a priceless opportunity for reflection, reminiscence, and celebration. What started, in most cases, as an armload of wiggling fur, needle-sharp teeth, and the elixir of puppy breath became a valued companion whose unconditional devotion and hunting skills enriched our lives both at home and, especially, in the field.

The lessons I have learned with, and sometimes from, the five gun dogs I've owned—four Labradors and one Irish red-and-white setter—have made me a better trainer, handler, and hunter. But lest we get too

Foreword

serious here, these dogs have also filled my home and heart with laughter and affection, sometimes when I needed it most.

To be sure, the stories in this book, *Empty Collars,* will make you sad, as they did me. But I hope that they will also remind you in a joyful way of the extraordinary quality of the bond we develop with our gun dogs, past and present. I hope that for you, like me, they will rekindle memories of special moments such as this one, which took place at the conclusion of my last hunt with a black Lab to whom I said good-bye not two months ago, after almost fourteen years together.

Side by side, Tad and I soaked up sight and sound like dry grass in a summer rain. As his big head swung to follow each group of wheeling birds, I knelt next to him and put my hand gently on the back of his neck, feeling the thick fur and heavy muscles that had served him so well for so long.

As we watched the ducks in the fading light, I tried not to think about the hard truth that we'd never see this sight again, he and I. And I succeeded.

Because sometimes, just sometimes, once is so good that once is enough.

Chris Cornell
Camden, Maine

Contributing Authors

JOE ARNETTE

TOM S. COOPER

GEORGE BIRD EVANS

CHARLES W. GUSEWELLE

DR. TOM HOLCOMB, DVM

ROBERT F. JONES

BEN HUR LAMPMAN

BILL McCLURE

CLIFF SCHROEDER

BILL TARRANT

MARK JEFFREY VOLK

DAVID WEBB

"Run a hand over that sensitive skull,

feel his understanding,

share his uncertainties, know his love—

and give him yours."

GEORGE BIRD EVANS

These Precious Days

GEORGE BIRD EVANS has enriched the lives of many readers by increasing their understanding of pointing dogs, and specifically English setters, for many years. Evans and his wife, Kay, established their own line, known as the Old Hemlock setters. The line was named after their place in West Virginia, located in the Allegheny Mountains near the Pennsylvania border. The couple moved to this location in 1939, and worked as a team, writing, illustrating, and photographing their experiences hunting grouse and woodcock with their setters.

Having written over twenty books, several anthologies, and many magazine articles, the late George Bird Evans has had and will continue to have a significant impact on his readers. His words have influenced, given enthusi-

Then these few precious days
I'll spend with you . . .
SEPTEMBER SONG
(KURT WEILL)

I have a letter from one of my Canadian readers telling me his thirteen-year-old golden retriever was losing his hearing and that his vet had also diagnosed failing vision due to cataracts. The man, with the Royal Canadian Police and scarcely a bleeding heart, was having difficulty accepting the fact that his dog would not be hunting with him in the coming season.

During a phone conversa-

asm for bird hunting with pointing dogs, and — of utmost importance, — provided ethics to the hunter in the pursuit of upland game.

An eleventh-generation Old Hemlock setter, Manton, now lives with Kay Evans, who gave permission for the use of three stories written by her late husband. "These Precious Days" originally appeared in the book, *Living With Gun Dogs*; "Char" was originally published *in The Pointing Dog Journal*, March/April 1995, and "The Last Indian Summer" was published in *Gun Dog* magazine, January/February 1986.

tion, a friend in the Midwest said the older of their two Old Hemlock setters would not be accompanying him to Michigan's Upper Peninsula on their regular shooting trip. At fifteen, she had been sitting out the last few seasons. (She lived to past sixteen.)

In *Seven Grand Gun Dogs*, Ray Holland told of leaving his springer spaniel, Little Duke, who was fifteen, at a boarding kennel together with his other dogs while he went to Cuba for the winter:

When May came and Dan and I went down to get the dogs, they were all in fine shape as they always were, but there was one dog less.

"He slipped away two days before Christmas," Will told me. Then he added, "I thought it was just as well not to tell you until you got home."

The situation was almost duplicated by a man I knew who left his old Brittany in a commercial kennel while he took his new young dog to gun quail in Georgia for the winter months.

Had the springer and the Brittany been my dogs, they would have been with me or I would have stayed at home with them. The only dog of mine to die without my hands on him was shot and buried to keep me from finding him.

It is easy to say that someday every young dog will be an old dog. Regrettably it isn't true. Of the nine setters we have had here at Old

Hemlock that are no longer living, only five lived into their thirteenth year or beyond. But when Fortune smiles on some gun dogs, as on some gunners, it is possible for them to go on living the shooting life to a remarkable age. I knew one setter who was past seventeen; his owner lived to be ninety-three.

I feel the act of hunting—both the exercise and the motivation— keeps men and dogs in vigorous condition. One of my Pennsylvania readers who regularly takes her setters to Georgia to gun bobwhites wrote:

> My hunting pal Barney is doing just fine at 12 years of age, and we are looking forward to the bird season.
>
> Thought you might like to know that my 103-year-old father is in great shape. He recently broke 74 blue rocks out of 100 at a shoot.

There can be no ignoring that circumstances can put an end to a dog's active life, but as long as it has been possible for them to enjoy it, Kay and I have given our older setters hunting, often limiting it to half an hour, but it was enough to have them feel they were needed.

Blue hunted long after he lost his vision from traumatic cataracts. Kay assumed the responsibility of keeping him in touch with coverts. He tended to wander up some hollow on a scent and get separated from Ruff and me. At such times he would sit and howl and Kay would go back and bring him to us. Often he would resist, feeling she was taking him to the station wagon, and she would have to lead him to us on a leash.

Some dogs lose both vision and hearing with age, making contact difficult, but with a bird dog's keen sense of smell they seem to manage better than humans. As if to compensate, Blue's loss of vision seemed to sharpen his hearing. He made some remarkable finds and retrieves of wing-tipped running birds, and he was especially happy when I hunted him alone, something the older dog should get to do occasionally, for it gives him the sense of responsibility of finding your birds for you. No dog should be regarded as a utility to be retired when he ceases to be useful.

One shot along Glade Run remains vivid in my mind. Blue and I were hunting, just the two of us, along a quiet stretch of the stream, and a grouse flushed under a thinning hawthorn loaded with yellow haws. At my shot it dropped in bracken in a little swale on the far side. My Fox still carried its original full and modified chokes, and when hit at twenty yards a grouse would usually be found where it fell. At ten years, Blue's vision was nearly gone, but to him a shot meant a hit—a less than accurate compliment—and he was in the area of the fall as promptly as if he could have seen the bird go down.

When I reached him there were still some barred flank feathers clinging to the coarse stems of the golden fern and I joined in the search, straining my eyes in the uncertain light of the glade. After a few minutes my original excitement became concern, and I laid my hat on the stiff bracken at the site of the fall and began circling around it. The prospect of losing a wounded grouse made me tense, and when Blue took this time to abandon the matter and wander upstream, I blew my whistle with unnecessary vehemence, which didn't improve my mood, but I got him back and searching once more near the barred feathers. It has been my experience that once a dog has assessed feathers on the ground he can disregard them with annoying nonchalance. After a second futile effort to make Blue seek I gave up on him when he moved off again, and began a crisscross pattern of my own. Had it been open forest floor it wouldn't have been so difficult, but the heavy bracken made a foot-by-foot search necessary.

The last I had heard Blue's bell had been at about forty yards, and now he was coming closer, swinging back, I supposed, to see what was keeping me. I could follow his progress by movement in the deep ferns, and then he pushed through with my grouse in his mouth, still alive and beating his face with its wings. Practically blind, he had trailed that running grouse in spite of my stupid intervention and he was sitting, presenting my bird to me with patient tolerance. I never saw his cloudy eyes look happier. It is moments such as this that keep the life flame burning bright for an aging dog—and his gunner.

My shooting notes for 14 October 1950 begin:

> Opening Day of grouse season, Ruff's fourth, my twenty-sixth, and Blue's twelfth, and I am almost certain it will be the last day Blue will have hunted.

It was cool and overcast with showers that kept moving over the wild Laurel Run country we were hunting. At first we moved nothing, trying to dodge squirrel hunters and the off-and-on rain. After eating lunch under a pine tree at the site of what had been a homeplace, we faced the fact that it was a matter of hunting in the rain or not at all.

Weakness in Blue's hindquarters had been progressing during the summer and today he was getting stiff and tired, although his lack of vision didn't seem to impede him other than his occasionally running into a low bush. While I made a big swing around the brink of the valley, Kay shepherded him in a shortcut across the top field grown to scattered thicket. Color was at its peak, each tree a separate beauty, each leaf a moment to be consummated, making up for the few grouse we had moved. The rain had lit the foliage to a fierce fire but it was so dense the two shots I had were like groping with a face full of leaves.

We were down in the deep valley, working our way upstream along big Laurel, when Blue simply sat down. Kay tried to coax him to keep moving but Blue had found a place that looked right and that was it. I was back there this season, forty years after, and those hills and that valley looked just as rough to me as they must have seemed to Blue.

Carrying a dog and a gun can't be done. I considered slipping my

Fox crosswise into the back of my coat with both ends protruding, but Kay insisted on carrying it, better than seven pounds of gun she wasn't used to.

Until you try to transport a setter held across your front like a baby, you can't realize how much he resembles a fifty-five-pound jellyfish slithering through your grasp with each step. Putting Blue on the ground, I crouched and with Kay's help got him draped around my neck like a blue belton fur piece. Once I was erect with my weight balanced, we made slow progress, with Blue accepting my swaying steps as calmly as a maharajah on an elephant.

We had an interruption when Ruff froze on his third lovely point of the day, one I couldn't fail to honor. I put Blue on the ground, took my gun from my gun bearer, loaded it and walked in, but the grouse gave me no chance to shoot. I once more got Blue across my shoulders and our procession proceeded. The rain let up just before we reached the station wagon, tired and soaked.

A hot bath and dinner made things right, and Kay and Blue and Ruff were drowsing before the fire by the time I had finished writing my notes. I was correct in my judgment that it would be Blue's last day under the gun, although he lived until the end of March 1952. He had been cheated out of the best of Life during the years of World War II, as were Kay and I with the exception of a couple of hunts on leave back at Old Hemlock, but even then we made the best of the situation. We gave Blue as much of the shooting life as we could, and he lived it fully. And that is all any of us can ask.

Like chiaroscuro in a painting, the lights and darks of happiness and sadness make Life deeper. Of all our setters here on Old Hemlock, Ruff had more of the golden days. He lived the longest, almost equaling his brother Clown who became a legend hunting bobwhites at past sixteen within his own ideas of exertion on Tallokas Plantation near Quitman, Georgia.

I think of certain days in Ruff's last and fifteenth season in 1961. At fourteen and a half, he was in remarkable condition, having outgrown episodes suspected of being *petit mal* three years earlier, which were evidently blood sugar insufficiency, not uncommon in dogs. To forestall such attacks as he grew older, we were careful to hunt him for short periods, often at end of day when we had brought the other dogs back to the car.

On November 2 we were gunning the beech cover partway up Cabin Mountain above Canaan Valley. It was lovely weather and we reversed our usual order, starting Ruff with Dixie, to loud protestations from Shadows in the station wagon. Two grouse flushed from a thicket of whip-size beech almost immediately, and we followed them south along the steep mountainside. One of them came back over me and I missed too soon with a left-crossing shot that could have been made with a little restraint.

We failed to move the second bird and doubled back at a higher level where the previous season we had seen two cock grouse fighting on the edge of the Forest Service road—a brace that would have been dead birds had certain hunters I know who gunned that area been where we watched from our station wagon. Today a big grouse flushed from a roadside brush heap and came over me from above. Like the last shot, I got on it too soon but managed to swing past, firing. The bird dropped, fluttering violently from a head shot as it rolled down the steep hillside, thrashing up tan beech leaves as it went. Ruff reached it first, making a lovely retrieve and sitting proudly to deliver a grand black-ruffed cockbird. He made more than a hundred and seventy such deliveries in his shooting life, but each one seemed to mean more to him and to me in his last year.

We returned to the station wagon and drove the incredible grade to the top of Cabin Mountain and out the crest to the end of the road where we wanted to give all three setters a turn around the knob. There was a parked car and a hunter coming out of the cover and I got caught with a long monologue while I chafed to get going for those last minutes before the sun went down.

Giving up, we turned back and Kay drove the road in short segments while I hunted Shadows on the lower side with no action. Near the gap I hunted the upper side on the principle that if birds weren't below it might mean they had moved higher as the sun was lowering. Suddenly a grouse was coming at me so directly it was a mere brown globe with wings. I let it go over and turned and dropped it going away high. Shadows must have been into others, for he didn't come to my shot or to my whistle. Concerned that the grouse was only winged and might run in the thick laurel, I called to Kay on the road below me to release Ruff and Dixie. Dixie was there almost before the car door slammed and retrieved a hen with a broken wing as I suspected.

To her consternation I hid the grouse before Ruff arrived. After a short search he found and brought it to me, delivering it sitting in full ceremony. I am certain he could get scent of Dixie's saliva on the feathers but in these dramatizations he invariably pretended he had made the original retrieve. The secret of enjoying Life is sometimes a little romantic make-believe.

Eight days later I started hunting a wild valley in my home coverts with Dixie, leaving Shadows to do yeoman duty keeping Ruff company in the old Country Squire station wagon. At three years, Dixie was coming into her prime and we found four grouse in the first twenty minutes. I heard a fifth go out at a distance, and within the next hour we moved #6, #7, and #8 on the upper edge of an old top field. Following one of them, I had a nice point from Dixie tipped over on the steep slope among sumac. Dr. Norris had died in February and I was shooting his little Purdey with all the warm memories it evoked. Its safety felt a bit strange to me but I had a good look at the grouse as it topped out among trees and at my shot it tumbled down the hillside. Dixie found and retrieved a lovely cockbird. I wonder if I will ever forget Dr. Norris's *Sometime when you shoot a big cock grouse, think of me.*

I was still in the hilltop clearing as I hurried around the shoulder of the ridge to get Ruff and Shadows before the sun went down, when grouse #9 flushed, and a moment later, #10. It came over me flaring up the hill and I wheeled and shot and saw it drop. Dixie got to it before its thrashing wings had stilled and was bringing it to me on the run. Ruff used to try to make his retrieves last long, Shadows delivered seriously and at the same time grinning, but Dixie always seemed to want to run to me with her bird.

Curiously, with all that action I remember a small ravine we followed down the side of the ridge. Walking briskly with the pleasant weight of two grouse bumping my back in my game pocket, something on the ground blending with the dead leaves caught my eye. It was a dried snakeskin on the leaf pack and I took time to examine it.

There were the shells of rattles on the tapered end, which meant that a rattlesnake with a newly minted skin was somewhere in the area, and I got Dixie out of there promptly.

It was a long trek to the station wagon where two eager setters waited, and after fortifying myself with a bite of food, I left Dixie in the rear compartment licking herself and trying to get the excitement sorted out in her mind.

Casting Ruff and Shadows, I headed into the lower portion of the valley. I was interested in dog work, not shooting another bird, and we moved two grouse almost immediately. In the gathering dampness of end of day scent lies well, and Ruff pointed one of the two on the follow-up, a good solid find with Shadows backing. Failing light turned us back when we had not much more than got started. I suppose it was well that something put a limit on my efforts to give Ruff his small share of every afternoon after having hunted hard those days during his last season, for I nearly wore myself out trying. It was at the end of that year that I was diagnosed as having hypoglycemia, and looking back I think it was probably the stimulus of all those grouse that kept me going.

Returning along the stream with its tumbling white water, we had still another flush. With my two birds in the car, there was an immeasurable sense of possession about leaving these others in that giant valley swallowing the night. My notes for that day end with:

> Marvelous day. Moved 12 grouse for 19 flushes-
> 5 shots, 2 hits, 1 productive and 2 retrieves by Dixie,
> 1 productive by Ruff, 1 backpoint by Shadows. I wouldn't
> tell my own mother about this place.

On the twenty-fifth of November Kay and I left Ruff and Shadows in the station wagon and hunted Dixie solo in one of our rugged mountain coverts above a fast trout stream so far below we couldn't hear the water pounding. It was a day that had been less than cold but was cooling in the shadows as we returned to the car.

We had hunted later than we had intended and as we crossed the plank bridge with the reflected chill of the rushing water I realized I could only let Ruff and Shadows out long enough to stretch their legs before starting the long drive home.

I let them sniff the grouse I had shot—the original 55 percent right barrel of the Purdey had a wicked bite and had decapitated this one at close range. While I was casing the gun and out of his sight changing my boots, Ruff got the impression I had gone hunting without him and set off on our backtrack.

We started down the woods road to the stream, whistling and calling, but the roar of the water drowned our voices. Returning to the car I sounded the horn and we once more walked down the path. As we neared the stream we saw him coming toward us, soaking wet and gaunt but undaunted. I still shudder to think of him swimming the high water below the bridge into the water; one thing was certain, he'd been in the stream all the way to his nose.

We got him in the car and rubbed him down with paper towels, then warmed him under the heater on the drive home, and he was well over it by the next morning except for a stiff neck.

One day in that final season, Ruff and Shadows were quartering a steep slope ahead of me when a grouse flushed wild to one side of Shadows. I watched as Ruff, unaware of the sound, approached the area of the flush. He caught the scent and went on a stunning point, wheeling to one side at the place where the grouse had lifted. Shadows, who had seen the flush and knew as well as I that the grouse had gone, froze in a loyal backpoint, honoring his sire. I gave the low whistle I had always given to Ruff to tell him I saw his point and he held, the muscles of one leg quivering with tension. I stepped in front of him, going through the motions of walking up the grouse and, making an imitation of a flush sound, sent him on. It was a small thing but it made him happy.

These Precious Days

Toward the end of that season that neither Ruff nor I would admit was going to end, I had him with Shadows in an excellent covert near home. The previous day Dixie had cut both wrists on broken glass in someone's lovely trash dump and had to be laid up. We came out on a back road, but instead of taking it, both Shadows and Ruff continued up the valley. It was a good impulse. In a clearing with an isolated crabapple thicket, I was mentally, and actually, going through a dry swing on a phantom grouse I pictured flushing from the copse, when Shadows circled from above with a premonition of scent. A grouse exploded and flared, offering me an incoming quartering shot against blue sky. My eyes locked on it and I fired swinging through, tumbling it from a cloud of feathers that hung on the cold air, a replica of the shot pattern, while the dead grouse somersaulted fifteen feet and landed on the snow. Ruff almost got there in time, but Shadows was a hard retriever to beat and he made the delivery with flair, a yearling cockbird nearly "boned" by the centered shot.

During Ruff's last years I made a ritual of hiding any bird another dog retrieved, letting him find and bring it to me. He went through these pretend retrieves with pleasure, partly I suspect to please me the way I tried to please him.

The dogs and I crossed to the far side of the stream, hunting in the direction of the station wagon. In the bottom Shadows swung like a compass needle and zeroed on scent, headed toward me. Ruff backed at my command but there was no flush when I walked in. There have always been these strange situations when dogs were working grouse, ghost points when scent is hot but with no bird there. It is "against the rules" to point ground scent, and yet some of the best grouse dogs utilize it to handle scary grouse and I don't quibble.

This bird was obviously nearby and both dogs moved on cautiously at my two-note mouth whistle. It was that last quarter hour of the day that minute-for-minute probably holds more chance for a shot than any other. As if to prove it, Ruff pointed and this time Shadows backed, but once more my mounting tension was left hanging with incompleted action. I gave Ruff the two-note go-on whistle but he refused, which held Shadows. I had taken twenty steps downstream when the blast-off came, a rustle of rhododendron foliage and a split-second glimpse of the grouse well out that at my shot became the bird fluttering down, winged.

Both dogs were running in at the report, steady-to-wing be damned. I had marked the fall in a small opening with frozen weeds. Shadows was searching beyond us when Ruff on my right almost stepped on the grouse, which darted behind him. He grabbed for it, missed, but in a moment had it, pinning it with his paw. Then with a firm grasp over its back, he delivered it, his age-silvered muzzle a lovely contrast to the black-barred breast of the bird. It was a yearling hen and I dispatched it as quickly as I could. Such moments are tainted by an awareness of the bird's valiant efforts to escape, putting me in the position of the intruder in a wilderness I want so much to be a part of. Ruff and Shadows weren't letting foolish thought intrude on a memorable experience, and we took time to do a lot of sniffing of feathers. When we reached the station wagon we had been out four hours, too long for Ruff but he showed no ill effects.

Ruff's final hour of glory came on a snowy New Year's Day in the Wildcat Rocks, a point on grouse that I described in "A Box of Shells" in *The Upland Shooting Life.*

We still didn't let that toll the end of his long life on birds. In February we took him with Shadows and Dixie to the newly opened Nemacolin Trails Shooting Preserve in nearby Pennsylvania. The big Reeves pheasants they were using at that time were a strange bird to grouse dogs and to me, but Ruff made a holiday of it, reminiscent of his days on Amwell, Dr. Norris's pheasant club.

In March we got training quail for Dixie, and at fifteen Ruff worked them with all the éclat of his young daughter. He was enjoying them ten days before he died on May 10, 1962. Ruff's was a long life fully lived. He didn't die of any illness, he simply died of living, fortunate in that he was hunting to the end. That I could be so lucky.

We gave Shadows the same sort of rich days in his last years. I am convinced he would have lived as long as Ruff had it not been for the trauma to his nervous system from the rifle bullet that plowed through his back in March of 1961. That he survived six years in spite of ensuing seizures was incredible. Toward the end we had to limit his hunting, but his intense pleasure never diminished, and I have precious memories of those hours with him and his devotion to me and our gun.

Dixie lived four years after Shadows, and we gave her hunting as long as she was able. I suppose you could say that she grew old in her thirteenth season, but to me it never seemed that she did.

I think it was with Briar, and later with Belton in almost identical circumstances, that the final season was so difficult and yet so sweet, knowing we were losing them but spinning out the days to the last strand. Briar, and again Belton, set us an example of courage throughout their ordeals, and always there was that comforting conviction that neither knew the implication of death, a dog's beneficence not granted man.

I don't feel that reflexes diminish to a great degree with age in either dog or man. Vision and hearing problems take their toll in shooting efficiency but the experienced gunner compensates with skill gained with the years. More than man, the gun dog calls on an amazing scope of sensory capacity during his lifetime, and at the end makes use of it in lieu of pure physical drive. But just as the older gunner clings to his confidence in his shooting, the aging dog needs the certainty that he still possesses his old brilliance in bird work. As Ruff encountered difficulties with the years, I wore a near-white shooting jacket to make it easier for him to see me and attached a dog bell to my belt to help him keep me located. Kay and I made every effort to bolster his assurance, seeing to it that he had more than his share of the retrieves.

Older dogs are sometimes subject to moments of confusion. When I let Ruff out at bedtime on the night of January 5 in 1962, he disappeared. He had been hunted nearly three and a half hours that day and three hours the day before; they were the final days of the season and I wanted to give him every last bit of hunting, but I had overdone it. Kay and I were worn to the bone, having gunned five days that week, but we got in the car and drove the back roads hopelessly searching for Ruff until 4:00 A.M. We found him—when we returned home, calmly lying under the hemlocks, and there was no way we could learn where he had been. There is little doubt in my mind that such episodes are related to blood sugar drop brought on by fatigue.

It is a bitter but lovely thing we know in the last years of our gun dogs, a period Kay and I have always tried to make a happy one. Savoring your dog's experiences on birds more than your shooting, you can give him much when he is old. During that time he spends long hours of his day in sleep, dreaming of hunting, but he needs so badly the stimulation of doing more than dreaming.

Those of us with highly developed sensibilities get much from Life, but in turn Life takes much out of us. Living with these wonderful beings we call gun dogs, we pay the awful price when they go. Whatever you call it—Providence, Fate, God—it is a less than kind deity that deals these blows. I should have had enough experience with it to accept it with less pain, but I know I never will.

It is not whether you and your dog have aged—Time takes care of that—it is whether the two of you have aged well, grasping every season, every day, extracting the juices and the ecstasy of your short time together. In his *Maximes* (1665), François Duc de La Rochefoucauld reflected upon the gradual loss of senses—hearing, sight, taste, touch, the ability to walk, to make love. "But," he added, "it is surprising how well we get along without them."

But Rochefoucauld was not a shooting man devoted to gun dogs. There may be certain limitations to the relation between a gunner and his dog, one of them being that there is an end. But total gratification is not the sole property of Youth. The aging shooter and the aging gun dog know a joy that is especially theirs—these precious days that come only after years with each other.

And when the leaves tell you it is Indian summer, make the most of it, don't fear it. Your old dog doesn't.

Char

Midway through this past grouse season Kay and Manton and I went back to the Pine Creek coverts of the Tiadaghton Forest of north-central Pennsylvania, with the new/old pleasure of returning to a great grouse terrain but with a wincing memory of Quest, where he had been so happy the year before. On the map it shows as mostly green forest land with designations such as Black Ash Swamp, Tamarack Swamp, Pine Creek Gorge, and with almost no town place names.

We had first gunned it the previous season—a wondrous land of nearly straight-up mountains channeling Pine Creek and its tributaries that come off the mountainsides like water chutes. You couldn't make up a world like this; you couldn't even dream it—titan peaks that soar above Pine Creek.

Unless you don't have good sense, you don't hunt those mountainsides of mature hardwoods with white pines and hemlocks that seem to have sifted down to the edge of the river. To find grouse you drive ten or fifteen miles up narrow white-knuckle Forest Service roads that hang on the mountains with much thin air on the off-side. There are unreassuring signs stating NO GUIDE RAILS and you try to keep your car on the inside away from the sheer drop. Kay, who was driving, announced, "If we meet a car, I'm stopping. He can do the passing."

Char

The small streams that pour off the mountains don't flow, they foam. I could picture lovely brook trout in those boulder pockets if you could reach them. These feeder streams form the dark waters of Pine Creek down below.

This was logging country in the days before the timber men moved southwest into West Virginia, defoliating the ridges like swarms of gypsy moths. I am told that early accounts described white pines up to two hundred feet tall with diameters of twelve feet growing in these valleys, together with some hemlocks with girths of twenty feet. How the loggers got them to the river to float downstream is hard to visualize, but they managed it with the same stocky Shay locomotives they used in our Blackwater/Canaan. The incredible destruction left by the slashings and forest fires created ruffed grouse cover that produced grouse on an enormous scale.

All that was then. What concerned me now was searching out residual grouse on the mountaintops.

There are clearcuts on the high flats and some game land plantings, and we found grouse in native regrowth white pines of moderate size. Kay and I came to one area like ghosts of an enchanted forest long since dead. Huge white pines had been cut so long ago the tops of their desiccated gray stumps were now jagged crowns. Ghoulish white birches, some twelve or more inches in diameter, had grown on top of the tombstone stumps and run their long fingers of roots down over and into the ground in a smothering grip that somehow seemed related to the death of the pines, if a dead stump can die again.

Shortly afterward, Manton gave us a point and I waited, ready for the shot while Kay moved up for a picture. She ran out of film after one exposure and had to reload, while I stood watching Manton immobile except for his intake and exhale of scent and my girl-photographer made the change, and I wondered how many dogs would hold like that. I didn't get the shot but Kay got a good one of the point tableau.

This is a kingdom of Indian names, taking you back to a time when there was no need for an alphabet—only sounds the white man tried to capture in his own spelling. Tiadaghton and Tioga fall musically on the tongue.

Our hosts this year were the same two friends who had us up for last season's hunt, each with orange belton half-sister daughters of Quest—Old Hemlock Sonnet and Old Hemlock Brooke. Both dogs knew that country well, an area difficult to gun without a companion familiar with the coverts.

An interesting part of our 1993 trip was meeting an elderly English setter named Char who belonged to Debbie and Tom Finkbiner, the proprietors of the Slate Run Store on Pine Creek. It is a landmark in this remote section—a modern rural general store, unpredictably combined with a large Orvis tackle shop. Neither Debbie nor Tom, a charming couple who are part of this setting, appeared surprised when we said it was Char we had come to see.

It was a rainy day that had kept us out of coverts, and we found Char in their small office, sleeping under the desk. He was in his thirteenth year, a lightly ticked blue snow belton about the size of our Old Hemlocks, looking—there was no other word for it—venerable, lying there unaware of our presence.

Char, a fitting name in this great trout country, opened one eye at Tom's voice, not mine, an aging gun dog like a fine old gun, dearer for being old. Kneeling beside him with my hand on his shoulder, feeling his tired breathing and the bony frame under the thin skin, I could see it all again, what Time had done to those of our Old Hemlock setters we had been fortunate enough to keep to such a ripe age, golden years when you live in their past with them.

Looking at Char as though he were something fragile, Tom was telling about getting him in the spring of 1981 from a litter in Williamsport, amid hundreds of square miles of what was once fabulous Pennsylvania grouse country.

Char

If you wonder why certain areas have produced great grouse dogs, it is partly because there were grouse there for them to work on and partly because they were bred from the dogs that had that experience.

Tom, who for years has hunted the rough terrain of Tioga and Lycoming Counties, brought Char up the way a grouse dog should be reared—on grouse. The two of them lived the one-man-one-dog life in complete devotion to each other. In the 1991 season Tom had to carry Char out of the woods. He didn't want to quit, but it was the last day he hunted. Tom has not hunted since.

Each of us who owns an aging bird dog shares a sense of impending loss with the gunner whose dog has come to the end of his hunting, and that rainy November afternoon we left Char still lying in his special place under the desk, knowing the chance of seeing him again was unlikely.

On our return this past November I intended to stop at the Slate Run Store but with each day I put it off. Having lost our Quest in April I dreaded hearing what I felt certain we would hear, realizing it was only a matter of learning when it had occurred.

On Saturday, our last day, we gunned a covert high in the limberlost of those ridges. Driving up the mountain, we passed camps with names like Antlers and Beulah Land, alive now with hunters in for the opening of the three-day bear season on Monday.

Brooke and her man had been forced to leave on Friday because of motor trouble in their Jeep. Sonnet's man, a minister of a large church in central Pennsylvania, had an appointment with his clergy Saturday evening and was going to take off in midafternoon after getting us started hunting. I was going to miss him—he was the lucky member of our party, seeming to exert a magnetic attraction for grouse. It might have been Sonnet's way with birds, but I consider it nothing less than Divine favoritism.

It was striking cover, this place he took us, with intermediate-to-small white pines among much mountain laurel and masses of wood fern frosted burnt sienna that seemed to appeal to grouse.

Our companion turned back about three o'clock, the diminishing tinkle of Sonnet's bell accenting the enormous quiet around us, broken by the murmur of the wind in the pines and the rasping throat rattle of two ravens soaring above us.

Manton worked the cover with his endless energy, but with the perversity of grouse, what birds there were were at the end of the big covert, leaving us a long way from our station wagon with the sun touching the treetops.

Manton and I had followed a grouse down into thick evergreens and had come back to where Kay was waiting on the trail. In mid-November the day goes down early and the white ball of sun was well toward the base of the bare trees when we started in that direction. The trail was through good cover all the way and I let Manton have his time, probing the sides, seeking like his sire, always questing. At one time I saw him pointing on the trail ahead and I was surprised how dim he appeared. I heard the grouse lift—mere motion as it crossed the path—and I almost tried for it, but I paced it and sixty yards would have been a fool's try.

Small white birches were visible now only as slender phantoms against the black-green of hemlocks, and we had gone to taking long steps with exaggerated pelvic action like marathon walkers. There was no question about getting out but I didn't relish the prospect of feeling for footing on this rocky path in darkness. Finally a less dark area loomed ahead and became the clearing with our station wagon looking pleasantly familiar.

Manton was ready to get into his rear compartment, and our headlights cut into total darkness as we drove down the narrow mountain road. There was the tinge of regret that comes with the end of the last day of a hunting trip—memory of the anticipation there had been at the beginning, which I couldn't help comparing with that of the bear hunters streaming in when we reached the paved road, all moving in the same direction.

We stopped at the Slate Run Store to fuel up for our trip home tomorrow, at least that's why I said we stopped. It was a lighted oasis of a country store on a Saturday evening, with parked vehicles and an overflow of hunters standing about in camp clothes. Kay went inside ahead of me, and after a boy filled our tank with gas I left Manton aroused from sleep and peering out the tailgate window at the action, and I faced what had drawn me there. For a year, an old gun dog wouldn't let my mind be at ease, seeing him as I had seen him last, lying the way old dogs lie halfway between sleep and death.

As I worked my way through groups of men I became aware of a shape in the night, backlighted by illumination from inside the store—a white form with a wagging tail. I heard a hunter telling where he had moved a bunch of grouse and I pushed past as though he weren't there. Char was standing at the roadside a few yards from me, barking not at anything in particular but simply at the night, just for the hell of it.

As I drew close I could see that he couldn't hear me speaking his name. With a wonderful surge of relief at the sight of him, I restrained an impulse to throw my arms around him, for fear of alarming him into moving into the headlights of the passing traffic.

He wore no collar to grasp and he resisted when I tried to pull him away by the back of his neck, feeling the bony scapula under the loose hide. His head was canted to the right side as though from a paralysis, and he staggered under my attempts to move him, but the tail was still wagging and that hoarse old-man's bark continued, seeming to rejoice in the gala mood of the hunters and the night.

Leaving the old boy where he was, for the simple reason I couldn't budge him, I went indoors to get Tom. I found Kay talking to Debbie amid a confusion of a store-full of hunters laying in provisions for the coming week. Kay had seen Char on her way in, and Debbie was saying: "I think he'll still be around when our obituaries are published."

Tom was coming in from outside, with Char walking calmly at heel.

"We're delighted to see you still have him," I said, flinching at the awkwardness of my words. "I found him on the edge of the road but I couldn't move him."

Tom laughed. "He's never gone onto the road, but I worry that some car might back over him in the parking lot. He can't hear a thing."

When I asked about the position of Char's head, Tom said it was the result of an inner ear infection the previous winter. "It left him with a balance problem and he tries to compensate, but for an old man he does pretty well."

Char was lying now at Debbie's and Tom's feet, drifting off to sleep. Seeing him like that, older than Quest lived to be, brought a hurt reminder of what we had lost.

Driving out the next day on our way home, we stopped at Slate Run and Tom brought Char out for Kay to get some pictures in daylight. There is a devotion in the way Tom handles him, helping him keep his balance, speaking to him as "Old Man."

Years ago I gave my heart to English setters before I was old enough to realize what total capitulation was, and it has been that way for eighty-eight years. When we have been blessed with gun dogs, we live as many lives as we have had dogs—each dog's years making up a separate life for us. There is a price to pay with each of them, for like our own, our dog's life has an ending, but you try to hold it back in the way you live the few or the long days together.

There is a postlude to this story. I called Tom and Debbie from Old Hemlock on New Year's Eve to ask about Char. Tom said Char had been losing weight and getting weaker, finally refusing to eat the kidney-failure diet he had been on.

"On Christmas Eve I decided something had to be done," Tom said. "The vet had warned me that meat would kill Char, but to tempt him to eat, I offered him some of the beef we had for dinner. He ate ravenously and couldn't seem to get enough. Since then, he's been devouring quantities of food—six cans of dog food one day. He's put on some weight and his hindquarters seem less weak. He's still tottery but his spirit is brighter and his eyes have the old-time look." Tom paused. "Whatever happens, his quality of life just wasn't worth living."

It brings to my mind a one-act play I saw in my bachelor days in New York in the Twenties. It was called *Old English* with George Arliss, that grand old actor playing an octogenarian bon vivant limited to pills and an intolerably stringent diet. In revolt, he has dinner served in his quarters—just the single character at a small candlelit table on center stage. The food was all those things he was forbidden—a partridge with two wines, a blazing plum pudding, a pot of black coffee, and finally a Havana panetela and a snifter glass with Napoleon brandy. Even the title, *Old English*, is an irresistible analogy. But for the sake of Char's peace of mind, I'm not telling how the play ended.

Seeing an old dog reaching an end, you die a little with him, even if he is not yours. A gun dog creates his own small eternity, and from a puppy, Char lived his years in the Pine Creek coverts. No matter when the inevitable comes, he will still be there like those mountains, for as long as Time and the river flow.

The Last
Indian Summer

A gunning trip to Maine—all those woodcock, those pa'tridge in old orchards—was a dream Kay and I had had for years. In 1978 we set it up.

One of my readers sent me copies of his topographic maps marked with luscious Xs where he was finding grouse in his Maine coverts—greater love hath. . . . A friend in Camden with two Old Hemlock setters turned his house over to us for a week while he and his wife would be in the West. Another friend with an Old Hemlock setter in western Massachusetts arranged for a cabin for us to stop over and gun grouse with him in the Berkshires. Our minds were full of visions of coverts like Lassell Ripley paintings, and both Briar and Belton caught the excitement in our voices.

Briar had been carrying what seemed a harmless condition that lit up the lymph glands in his throat, a situation that became more acute while we were in Massachusetts. Through still another friend, an MD who also has an Old Hemlock setter, we obtained an appointment with a specialist at the Angell Memorial Hospital in Boston.

We were given the diagnosis on an October day in one of the most beautiful Indian summers of my life. It was as though the world had ended.

The Last Indian Summer

The Angell is a top referral animal hospital and we couldn't indulge in the consolation of doubting their opinion. "Six months; with luck, maybe seven," the specialist had said, and our first trip to Maine became a turnabout and retreat to Old Hemlock, as though that could make it different.

On the long drive home, remembering Briar's gallant air as we watched him being led to biopsy surgery at Angell by a girl attendant, remembering how he had turned his head from side to side to examine the strange milieu, curious but not disturbed, Kay and I gathered a little of his courage and got our thoughts in order. We would fight this thing—we had the prescriptions and detailed directions to pass on to our vet for the chemotherapy—and we would keep Briar with us for as long as Time would be kind. We would give him his last season as fully as it would be possible for him to enjoy it, and we vowed not to tarnish its glory by imparting a sense of our anxiety.

ɬ ɬ ɬ

We reached Old Hemlock on October 18, faced with a short period of waiting until our vet could obtain the prescribed medications. We were in touch with the specialist in Boston and with her approval, started our home season on the twentieth in one of our woodcock coverts in the high bog country, driving up the gap through gorgeous autumn color. Foliage was persisting two weeks late, but leaves were thinner on the higher elevations, with hawthorns loaded with red and yellow haws, and large blueberries withered and dried on crimson bushes. The weather was autumn perfect, and Briar hunted one and a half hours. We found two grouse and two woodcock with no shots, but Briar worked in a state of delight with no hint of tiring, his face and attitude showing how much it meant to him, hunting with all his old seriousness.

When we thought Briar had enough, Kay led him, not without duress, to the car where she waited with him while Belton and I took another turn. My gun diary entry ends: "If we can give Briar this much this season, I'll be happy. And there is no slightest doubt that Briar is."

Five days later we were in two of our favorite woodcock coverts on Big Allegheny Mountain. My diary reads:

> *The Glorious Twenty-Fifth,* the date of the flights. In deference to Briar's condition, I took Belton alone in the first covert and Kay and Briar remained in the car at the abandoned Poplar House sleeping away its years. Belton and I found two 'cock—no grouse—and rejoined Kay and Briar at 4:45. We drove the car at a crawl up the stony mountain road, dragging on rocks, and it took half an hour to reach the plateau on top.
>
> Briar had his first chemotherapy yesterday and to our amazement was feeling fine today. He knows this big hawthorn flat and after a wild dash by both rascals, settled into hunting every good spot. With Belton on point deep in cover and Briar backing, the first woodcock flushed over the far thorns with no shot.
>
> I swung the dogs into cover on the edge of a huge boggy pasture and soon found Belton honoring Briar, who was solid in a small hawthorn clump with his soul in his eyes. When Kay reached me with her camera I walked in front of the point while she knelt low to give me the shot. The 'cock bored over Briar's head and took the far side of the thorns and I fired through dense twigs and missed. As I reloaded, Briar moved out hoping for a retrieve, but Belton held, now pointing scent. I flushed his bird—the second of the brace—and dropped it right-quartering and close. I was using the 50 percent-60 percent pair of Purdey barrels for the first time in years, shooting some old Alcan 3-1-#8 shells, a sweet load in these barrels.

Belton found the bird, pointed dead, and was about to pick it up when Briar came in and took over and Belton deferred to seniority. Briar made a hammy show of the retrieve, lying down with the woodcock, while we gave him his fun, then delivered it, a yearling male, for Kay's photo.

Our last cast was out to the "hedgerow cover," where we had three wild flushes with the dogs not near them. While Kay went for the car, I worked both dogs in a big circle. Briar made a point that both he and I thought would produce. He was in a stand of briars and locusts— nasty cover—where he seemed determined to create a bird that wasn't there. I at last persuaded him to leave and we met Kay on the road where she had stopped the car.

I took our single woodcock from my game pocket and let Briar nose it before I put it in the car. While we changed out of boots, he lay on the roadside in the damp fragrance and grinned with his tongue hanging out, a blood-red sun sinking through the filigree of hawthorn twigs behind him.

That image of him is etched on my brain, and I see it every time we come out of that covert, as I have seen it through the long years since we lost him. It was a grand afternoon, an example of what one little woodcock can give two splendid setters and two grateful people.

❧ ❧ ❧

A few days later we again drove to the high mountains for woodcock on a clear fifty-degree day. Briar and Belton had crossed a rail fence into woods not fifty yards from the station wagon when I saw Briar, low in front with tail up and Belton backing, in cover so dense I couldn't determine how to flush the bird. The 'cock lifted as

I circled below and I had to wait till it was well out to shoot and saw it fall.

Briar was over the rails and into high weeds searching and soon had the woodcock and delivered it, a large hen. It almost seemed that our anxiety for him had been a bad dream on our New England trip and that, now we were back home in our mountains, everything was going to be all right.

The following day we gunned "The Wilderness," one of our home coverts. My gun diary entry opens with *"Ein Heldensetzen! A hero setter! This was Briar's day."*

🌾 🌾 🌾

It is cover on a ridgeside, and we had hunted a woods road through grapevines hanging full of more grapes than I'd seen in many seasons, the silhouettes frosty blue against a sky like blue enamel. The leaves were just past their peak of color, a delightful time to be in woods with a brace of setters and a gun. Briar was full of pleasure, quartering each side of the path with as fine a ground pattern as I had seen him put down.

We made a big circle on two levels and were nearing the car without having moved a feather—so much for perfect cover and abundance of food as the sole factors for grouse. As we approached the car, both dogs went fragrant without a bird. With Belton working nearby, Kay and I climbed the slope and were unlocking the tailgate when we heard Briar bark treed some distance behind us in the thicket, and realized he had been pointing.

Turning, we saw a grouse perched in a bare maple, then saw another flush north and a third flush south. I moved toward Briar, with my eyes on the bird sitting tall in the leafless maple. Within seconds it pitched and I fired at a good thirty-five yards through a screen of branches and leaves. Neither Kay nor I saw it after the shot—only a scattering of leaves fluttering down like feathers.

As we fought through intervening greenbrier and dense saplings,

Briar, certain that I couldn't miss, began scouring the area ahead with Belton hard after him. With none of Briar's confidence in my shooting, I pushed on, following what I felt was the bird's line of flight.

Kay called that Briar was working scent excitedly and that Belton had joined him. When I got to them, both dogs were nosing down into crevices between large rocks. Belton moved farther out but Briar wouldn't give up, plunging his face deep underground with loud snuffling sounds. Kay found a grouse breast feather and we knew our bird was down there.

I unloaded my gun and laid it aside, then reached as far as I could into several of the openings, all of which extended beyond arm's length. While I tried to think of a solution, Briar started digging frantically and, inserting his muzzle, came up with the struggling grouse. Nothing is sweeter than seeing your bird under these circumstances, and I managed to take the grouse from Briar, dispatch it, and return it to him. He stood, grasping it in his mouth and grinning around it, while Kay and I hooted like idiots and Kay took yards of movie film.

When I at last accepted the grouse from Briar, I saw Belton, who knew better than to come near at a time like this, sitting at one side. My notes read:

> Belton is a grand young dog in this his third season, but what we witnessed was the master grouse dog at work, a blazing end to the day. Briar's grouse was a yearling cock without the "double eye" marking on the lower back feathers. Briar is so happy and seems well, and we are grateful for him, for this covert, and for that moment. I almost added, *Amen.* As I write this, once again "a grouse and a brace of woodcock hang on the hewn-log wall of the porch in the sherry smell of leaves, and Life is as I would have it."

It was, at least, for then.

We hunted Briar one more day, then took him to our vet for his second intravenous injection of Oncovin. On the way, we stopped for a short turn in a familiar covert and he pointed a grouse near a drumming log. We hunted two more days that week, with good work and several productive points by Briar, and one day we found a fair flight of woodcock.

After his third injection on November 7, Briar refused food. From the beginning of the treatment his weight had dropped from 65 pounds to 56½, and although we had been warned, we were deeply concerned. I rested him and slowly he regained a pound or two. My notes read:

> I stand, looking up into these golden maples and beg *Please don't go,* but even as I speak, the leaves keep falling down around me. Another Indian summer day—how many there have been, some terribly unhappy, but others, like today, so blessedly relieving, for Briar is once more on level and eating, but he is far too rundown and weak to exert in the woods.

On November 13 we had a good day in the Canaan Valley, and Briar was working like his own wonderful. self. We drove out of the covert after sunset in mist with a giant second Hunter's Moon full and golden, etched with the tops of large aspens where Kay and I and generations of Old Hemlock setters have had glorious days.

On November 22, five days after Briar's fourth treatment, we had a day's gunning that will forever be with us. We were in a favorite Pennsylvania covert in the big Youghiogheny River basin. Briar appeared in good condition but he seemed to hold to the paths more than normally, while Belton hunted the sides.

We were in the headwaters of a trout stream that had given Kay and me fishing in the old days. I saw Briar hit scent at an ancient sawmill site grown to goldenrod and weeds around the rotting sawdust pile, just as grouse began flushing. Birds #1 and #2 were mere sounds, #3 scaled across to a ledge of rocks, and #4 topped the trees on the slope above me—all too distant for shots.

Because of the spookiness of the grouse this season, I was working Briar and Belton without their bells, and the two dogs quartering in the total quiet of woods was lovely, with only the sound of their pads on fallen leaves. We had two reflushes before turning back to the small stream where we sat on a log to eat lunch.

Hunting toward the car to give Briar a rest, I saw Belton on point, high and handsome at the edge of dense rhododendron. Before I could reach him, a grouse exploded out of the thick cover and flew down the woods road beyond the car, disappearing at the bend a hundred yards away.

I left Kay to get Briar into the car and drive after me while I swung Belton down the road fringed with rhododendron. I found him on point in an offset on the left where I had lost sight of the grouse. I was approaching the point when Briar came dashing to me, having broken away from Kay, his momentum carrying him past.

Belton was faced away from me, his rear legs spread wide and his head turned toward a big rhododendron on the right. I saw him flinch and heard the grouse start and take the old road behind me, flying straight down the grade. I fired and it crumpled and fell fluttering in front of Briar fifty yards away.

Briar was on it in seconds, lost his grip and piled after it into laurel on the lower side of the road. Kay afterward told me she saw it all as she drove down the road—the flush, the shot, Briar's capturing the grouse.

He was standing below the road, guarding his prize and growling at poor Belton who was sitting watching pathetically as Briar mouthed his grouse. Before I could persuade the temperamental star to deliver the grouse to me, Kay had to remove Belton to the car.

Everything we had felt in all our shooting years, we felt more sharply now. Days like this had made our life; it was days like this that kept us going at this time.

After losing weight so drastically, Briar now began to gain, eventually weighing 68 pounds, more than he had ever weighed.

Following the deer season, we resumed hunting in December, limiting Briar to two hours. In one of my entries I wrote:

> Briar having worked one and three-quarter hours, Kay walked him back to the station wagon. Seeing the two of them going over the skyline, Kay leading Briar with frequent stops while he turned to look back at me, was heartbreaking. He has no way of understanding, but I do, so clearly.

We hunted Briar five days during the week of December 11. He seemed so eager I took him solo one day as a special treat. We came to an empty house on an abandoned farm with what had been the garden chest-high in frost-killed goldenrod. He plowed through it like a youngster, reaching a four-and-a-half-foot board fence at the far end that I thought would stop him. My diary has a sketch titled "The Old Dog," showing Briar going up-end over the top board. Flipping over, he went on hunting without losing a stride.

Briar's spirit did much to keep Kay and me from becoming despondent about his illness. A friend who has a nine-year-old Old Hemlock setter said, "I don't think I could handle that situation." My answer was, "Yes you would, Sam. You have to."

There were difficult days, times when Briar suffered reactions to the Oncovin injections and the other drugs. When heavy snows prevented our making the thirty-mile trip to our vet, I had to administer the injection while Kay grasped Briar's foreleg at the elbow to distend the vein. It was a harrowing procedure for me, knowing that a misplaced injection of Oncovin would destroy tissue and slough away flesh at the site of the puncture. One time I missed, and once it did.

Briar was heroic in his acceptance, watching my shaking hand and the needle with patient interest.

On January 19, the day before his tenth birthday, I gave Briar his ninth injection. On the twenty-third it was milder, and with the snow softening we tried hunting.

As we drew near the mountain we saw glistening surfaces on the upper portion of the ridge. When we turned into a side road on top we came to a glare of ice that sent us back to a lower elevation.

Hunting a log road that parallels the valley stream, we reached old fields growing to thicket where we had often found birds. Today there were not even tracks. But Briar was in a splendid mood and Belton was handling beautifully—a brace that was a joy to gun over.

Beyond the "marker hemlock" we ascended a log road I had never tried. Walking ahead of Kay, as we usually hunt in coverts, I came to an ice band, as distinct as if it had been sprayed on every tree trunk and stump and rock. I made the observation that there was no use expecting grouse in such conditions, but Kay suggested that, with plenty of time, we should explore it.

We found ourselves on what had been a wooded flat, recently timbered, with brush piles and a lacing of log roads. The openings were not yet choked with blackberry briars and the combination looked like perfection.

Briar and Belton were working along one of the log roads and from her view of them, Kay called that both dogs were looking birdy. We couldn't see a point, but both bells were silent and a grouse lifted beyond them and sailed down over the hillside. Suddenly I heard a second grouse flush and wheeled to see it crossing left-to-right about head-high and going fast. It was close but I instinctively swung through and fired just ahead of it. For a moment I thought I had missed, then the grouse folded and went down into boulders and brush piles below us, and I heard that wonderful sound from Kay.

Both dogs raced to me and I waved them over into the tangle, where

Briar soon got the line and disappeared. When he didn't show again, I knew he had it.

Climbing down on icy footing, we saw him below us to our left, standing with his head in the snowy brush, his tail wagging. We finally reached him for a movie of the retrieving ritual, with Belton close behind us.

The ritual became a spectacle as we waited and cajoled Briar, begging, demanding, ordering, and threatening while he glowered at Belton and deliberately pulled feathers from that lovely grouse. I should have taken it from him, but I wanted him to have that retrieve at his leisure.

He took time to growl again at Belton and even at Kay when she went to him and got him started toward me with the bird. He at last delivered it, a yearling male with exactly three very long tail feathers intact, both legs plucked bare, the primaries soaked, and much of the back plumage gone, but we made over him as if his retrieve had been feather-perfect, and he was delighted with himself. Kay's photo of the event shows Briar delivering the grouse with the day dying in the southwest under a sorrowing sunset reflected on sodden snow.

I wrote in my notes: "Next time I must intervene." There was no next time.

We moved up the ridge into the ice once more. Belton pointed and Briar came in and getting scent, went intense, his head reaching, his tail erect. My sketch of the two—an orange-and-blue-belton brace— bears the caption *High Voltage*.

From that January 23 to February 28, we were kept in by heavy snows. On the twenty-eighth, the Last Day, we went out in snow that was chest-high on the dogs, and moved nothing. It was Briar's last day under the gun. We had given him thirty-one days of gunning that last season and I think nothing could have made him happier.

Without the hunting, March was bad—bad weather, bad times for Briar, a month punctuated with weekly chemotherapy. By April, Kay and Briar and I were looking Death straight in the eye, and at least Kay and I knew it.

In that month we took Briar on two trips to the Canaan Valley, where we had the beneficence of returning spring woodcock. On the Saturday before Easter we were returning to the station wagon after finding no 'cock, not even whitewash, when I saw Briar in alders just beyond the big aspens where he had pinned so many woodcock for me. It was a gorgeous point, and he didn't move a hair during all the time it took me to approach. Before I got to him the bird flushed and came around to my left, its big fan spread sharply against the cloudy sky, a cock grouse where I hadn't seen a grouse for years, a holy moment for Briar and Kay and me. Up to this time I hadn't seen Belton, but now I heard his bell toll from out in the alders where he had been paying tribute to Briar's point. It was the last grouse Briar pointed in a lifetime of pointing grouse.

On May 2, Briar was working bobwhites released for him on Hunting Hills Preserve. He was very run-down but happy, intense and honest on every point, magnificent to the end.

The trip to Maine ended under our hemlocks on May 10. During the hour I waited for the vet to arrive, my hands never leaving Briar's head, he opened his eyes twice, looking up at me. The question was as clear as if it had been spoken: *Why?*

Nothing is more desolate, more sadly happy than to give a dog his final season before losing him. Those last seven months were an exercise in courage, with Briar leading Kay and me all the way. He had been gallant throughout his ordeal, making it possible for us to endure what seemed unendurable until we had gone through it, an Indian summer that lasted so long but went so fast.

Those who say a dog has no soul are defining *soul* differently than I do. Briar's soul is with me among these hemlocks needle-sharp against flaming sunsets, and will be for as long as I am here. For those of you who have lost a dog, you have my word that this is so.

BILL McCLURE

Not Forever—
Just a Lifetime

BILL McCLURE and his wife, Kathryn, live in a ruffed grouse covert near Manotick, Ontario. Bill has bred, trained, field-trialed, shown, and hunted with Brittanys for forty-five years. His current three females are line descendants of the first dog he and Kathryn owned.

A successful field trialer and judge in the United States and Canada, Bill has been a lifelong bird hunter. He and his dogs are in their favorite grouse and woodcock coverts more than sixty days each season.

By profession an outdoor writer and photographer, Bill wrote a column for *Gun Dog* and *Wildfowl* magazines for many years, and he continues to write about gun dogs for *The American Hunter* magazine (the National Rifle Association's monthly publi-

Spring 1985. Time for some good news. Time for puppies, fresh hopes, and fond memories of dogs and birds from seasons gone, not lost. Memories of your first dog or your best. Of the time when you hustled from point to point, flush to flush, or retrieve to retrieve. To the years then and now when few worried about enough birds or free space on which they could grow or upon which we could walk free of fear or worry. Back to the time when gunning meant more fun and less earnestness. Before "limit your kill, don't kill your limit" and pre-dating "quality hunt."

cation). In addition, Bill has contributed to many other publications.

The story, "Not Forever—Just a Lifetime," was originally published in the March/April 1985 issue of *Gun Dog* magazine. Permission to use the story in the anthology was given by Bill McClure.

Please, no slogan — it's springtime with drumming grouse, trilling woodcock, winnowing snipe, booming sharptails, melodious quail, and throaty partridge in every covert and grassland. The airborne have landed on the plains of Manitoba, Saskatchewan, and Alberta, radiant in their breeding costumes; black dots on the brown prairie sloughs.

Renewal. Wish them water in just the exact amount. Ten mustard babies—children of the plains filling the August skies with flying arrows. April. Brown to green. A grouse nests in the center of our dog graveyard. All twelve eggs hatch. It is warm and sunny, giving life to dead ground. Overhead the warblers applaud the trilliums.

Recollection. Oh, how the now still dogs once flew over the earth in headlong pursuit of the ancestors of those who now nest above their graves. 1964 and Kip, who sped across this very ground one golden day in friendly competition with a renowned bracemate, pointing twelve out of twelve grouse while the celebrated went birdless— unable to match the speed and unerring sense of location. Incredible. But the believing was in the eyes and now, the memories of the three of us who watched the unbelievable. Not one mistake nor hesitation. She went like the wind. Probing into it, and across it seeking that telltale aroma which arrested motion. Suspended. The condensing breath from her nostrils the only stirring until the wings. On that great day no shots were fired, but in other coverts and on other days the chase was joined. How we two loved it! Most often just the two of us, the birds, the golden days, the migrating geese high overhead, the robins chattering from the wild grapes, the blue, the corners that almost always held the bird, and the ones that were impossible to surround.

We two accepted with exchanged glances the impossible, celebrating the escape of a grouse that could be heard but never seen. Cursed but not unloved. They were always enormous; the smaller ones were in the game pocket warm against my back. At dusk we sat together, alert in the chill, watching the dark shapes of woodcock flit across the sunset to the brook-bracketed night cover. Tomorrow.

October tomorrows always came on time and with them the 'cock. They were there and still are. Kip's son, who rests beside her, that handsome little man who so proudly presented his near-perfect form in conformation shows, raced to meet them. At Dutchman's, Clubhouse, Stone Bridge, and all the other coverts he flew until the warm scent became hot and then he slowed and carefully stood the immobile October migrants. And once each season came the Labrador twisters that flushed when you crossed the fence, calling for whispered commands, steely nerves, and lots and lots of cartridges. When the twisters flushed, their next stop was South Carolina and they flew as if they were confident they would complete their journey. Most did.

King enjoyed woodcock shooting in the poplar groves, but found his mother's favorite grouse more than he could handle. None of us is perfect.

But his son Prince thought he was. So perfect that he shouted with joy when the leash was slipped and charged the old covers with wild confidence. Follow me to victory! Follow him I did for twelve short years. When I lagged a bit, he would rush back, stop and wait as if to say, "Quickly, this won't last forever." It didn't. It never does. But while it lasted it was exhilarating, for Prince was a chip off his grandmother's genes. He considered grouse big game, partridge a pastime, and woodcock nature's joke on bird dogs. He pointed woodcock but almost always jumped in to flush them when I drew alongside. As soon as the bird was up, he would stop and look back at me with an expression that I was always sure said, "Let's clear the coverts of these things and get on with the game shooting."

Grouse were different. Prince treated them with high tension, his posture, distended eyeballs, rigid tail capped with a trembling white tuft, all indicated big game. He too knew where they would most likely be and he rushed to the corners, inspected the arbors, and could smell an apple tree 200 yards away. When the great grouse fell, he brought them back as if in a trance, taking time after delivery to compose himself before seeking more encounters with his chosen medium. Prince was a fun dog, a good dog who brought to each day afield a sense of optimism and boundless joy that filled our hearts with memories to last all of our days. He was the guy who rounded up four grouse one November on Canadian Remembrance Day, and gave me one of the few opportunities for a double as three of the four went out at once on either side of the wild apple tree. And, for once, I was triumphant and my enthusiastic pal was near a coma as he had to retrieve two. I still tip my hat when I pass that place.

And I have passed it countless times with his daughter, but it was not there that Corky gave me my only other chance for a double on grouse, but at Dutchman's where her grandfather and great-grand-mother had sought grouse and woodcock. The grouse were in the grapes—probably drunk and reluctant to fly—but fly they did, simul-taneously in opposite directions through heavy vines and brush. To our mutual amazement both came down such a short distance from the truck that we just took the birds and hung them in the back and went over to see if there were any woodcock at home.

Corky was an accomplished switch-hitter who could cope with each species well. She had her ancestors' love for grouse and the patience to go carefully for the little birds. Her lifelong failing was an adoration for the snowshoe hare. Throughout her life this quarry took up considerable shooting time but apparently she thought it worth-while in spite of my disagreement—or maybe because of it. When not coursing hares or lying around the house with her treasured bleached white bone jutting from her face, our much loved lady pointed everything with wings. She was one of the "pointenest" dogs I ever owned. She was always embarrassed if anything from a sparrow to a pheasant flushed before she stood it.

From 1972 to 1983, I and my son, who loved Corky long and well, gunned over our fat dog. Blair took his first birds with her and, on one memorable Saturday morning at the Clubhouse covert, Corky rendered a dazzling 27 points; my seventeen-year-old and I were home for a late lunch with a lifetime of stories. (Blair claims to this day that my instruction before casting Corky away—into what I was certain was a bird bonanza—was, "Don't shoot the dog.")

Last summer we buried her beside her father. The house and our hearts are still empty. Corky passed her pointing propensity to her daughter who helped to elevate the autumn of 1984.

The Nick has eyes like a cougar, the reflexes of a jaguar, and the nose of a bird dog. She can see a nuthatch move fifty yards away even when she is running. I have never owned a dog who was so conscious of her environment. She can hear the can opener in our kitchen from her kennel run, twenty yards and one house wall away, and barks to arouse her roommate who is less attuned to the day's beginning. She simply adores bird finding and, not remarkably, considering her sensory development, is quite good at it. She is good at all of it— grouse, woodcock, partridge, and snipe. The latter, the most difficult of all for any dog to stand, have so far proven quite simple for The Nick. Like her mother, she has had a liking for hares, but has periods of reformation. I have built on her strengths and trusted her judgment.

And where else in North America can a gun dog enjoy the game-finding opportunities she has experienced here in Ontario? Of course, during her first two seasons of grouse, the population was very low, but there were lots of Huns, a reasonable population of woodcock, and snipe present and accounted for. So The Nick and I were gunning every day in October 1984 and on one busy day we were able to get pointed one of each of our local upland game birds. The good old days are still with us. We may not fill our hats like the gunners at the turn of the twentieth century, but can anyone in good conscience complain when you and your gun dog can get four species pointed in a few hours?

※ ※ ※

For The Nick and for most Canadian gunners and their dogs, the good old days stretch from there to now. When your current gun dog represents thirty years of pleasure afield with all her forebears, it is difficult if not impossible to look back with longing for what used to be. My nostalgia is for what was and can never be again, my joy is in the present, and the thrill is in anticipation of what is yet to be.

Caps are tipped at the wild red apple tree in the Clubhouse covert, a salute is given to the fence corner where the grapes still hang thick. A dead name is whispered as I vault the rusted fence to enter the woodcock glen at Dutchman's, and if I have a shooting guest I often have to bite my tongue to keep from disturbing the moment with memories of what her grandmother did one frosty morn in this very place. And in this place the woodcock will sing as they will in Quebec, New Brunswick, Prince Edward Island, and Nova Scotia. The grouse will drum this spring right across Canada and as they did in 1966 will rebound to decent populations from their present scarcity. If not this year, then next. There have always been grouse and probably always will be.

Once again a bird will nest in our dogs' graveyard. Maybe not exactly in the center of the ring of stones but close enough to remind us that April is a warming month, giving life to cold ground. It is springtime in Canada and time for some good news. It will not last forever, Princey, just one lifetime.

ROBERT F. JONES

My Girl Friday

The late **ROBERT F. JONES** was, as a colleague stated, "one helluva writer." He was Editor-at-Large for *Shooting Sportsman* magazine, and his "Dawn Patrol" column was a regular monthly feature. He was a prolific and well-traveled writer, having worked for *Time, Sports Illustrated, People, Life, Audubon, Men's Journal,* and many other publications. He authored seven novels and eight works of nonfiction.

Bob Jones had a passion for hunting what he considered the best of all gamebirds—ruffed grouse and woodcock. He started pursuing prairie birds in Wisconsin, hunted around the world, and for the past dozen years or so hunted his favorite upland birds in Vermont.

Permission to use two of his stories, "My Girl Friday" and "The Last Hunt," was given by his

I've owned pointers and setters in my time, and good dogs they were, but I finally settled on the Labrador retriever as my gun dog of choice. For thirty years now they've rewarded my loyalty with fine work and fast shooting on both waterfowl and upland birds, and I thought I'd never stray. I like Labs for their smarts, their steadiness, their calm dispositions, their desire to please, and the fire that blazes from their eyes whenever the game is a-wing. Secretly, though, I've always felt that any dog, regardless of race, creed, gender, or place of national origin, can be taught to hunt birds. All this is by way of explaining why now—

My Girl Friday

wife, Louise Jones. Both pieces were originally published by *Shooting Sportsman* magazine.

in addition to my superb yellow Lab, Kent Hollow Jake—I own the funniest, feistiest little bitch known to dogdom, a terror of a terrier named Rosalind Russell.

I got Roz as a puppy from my pals Joe Judge and Donna Davenport. Joe's a Chessie and Gordon setter man, but for a while he had a combative Jack Russell named Boomer, and acquired a bitch of the breed to provide him with a mate—Mrs. Boomer, known more familiarly as Mrs. B. The trouble was that Boomer always wanted to fight with his canine houseguests. Before Boomer could manage to get himself crunched, Joe dealt him off to a shooting friend, who later reported that Boomer had turned into a superb dove and quail dog. He'd sit steadfast with his new owner in a dove blind, mark down all the kills and cripples, retrieve them on command, and stack them neatly in little piles in the blind. On quail he worked close and flushed the birds as niftily as a springer spaniel—though he sprang even higher when he pounced.

Mrs. B. is no slouch as a hunter herself. Though she weighs only fourteen pounds, she prefers big game to birds. I was talking with Joe on the phone one evening when he interrupted the conversation to give me a blow-by-blow of Mrs. B. stalking an eight-point whitetail buck that was feeding on Joe's front lawn. "She's getting close now, belly down, ears back, he doesn't see her yet. . . . He's looking up, looking behind him. Christ! He whips around and runs for it, she jumps, grabs him by the ass—she's hanging on for dear life! There they go, into the cornfield, the bucktail wagging the dog. . . ."

That doesn't surprise me at all—nothing about Russells does. I had a friend back in the 1970s who had a Jack named Dudley. While visiting him one winter up in the Catskills, we took a walk in the snowy woods with our wives, with Dudley and his littermate, Bentley, frisking ahead of us. We hiked through ankle-deep snow along a frozen creek, the anchor ice light blue beneath the gelid sky, whole cascades frozen in place by winter's bite; and Stephen—an Englishman—said he'd been cataloging the winter with his camera (he was and is a superb photographer). As we turned back toward his home, we passed a house on the porch of which resided two large, black dogs—a Labrador and a Newfoundland. The big dogs came pouring off the porch in a hell of a fury. Dudley and Bentley kept their silence. They raced toward the big dogs with a steadfastness of purpose and such a murderous intent that the Lab and Newfie suddenly changed their minds about home guard duty. They galloped back to the porch. Dudley and Bentley sprang up the steps and backed the big dogs against the front door. The house's owner, a citified gent, then stepped outside and in high color yelled down to us, "Get those hell-hounds out of here or I'll call the police!"

Together the Russells weighed about twenty-eight pounds. The retrievers, two hundred.

🌿　🌿　🌿

Russells were originally bred by a nineteenth-century English parson, the Reverend Jack Russell, who rode fanatically to hounds. His dogs were derived from the fox terrier, and selected for courage, ferocity, speed, small size, and total toughness. They ran with the long-legged foxhounds—often thirty or forty miles a day—and when a fox went to ground, the Russell was sent down the hole to chase it back out. They also were dispatched into badger setts on suicide missions—kill or be killed—and usually emerged victorious, though sometimes lacking an ear or an eye.

In his heartwarming book, *Tales of a Rat-Hunting Man*, a tough Welshman named D. Brian Plummer defines the breed thus: ". . . the multitude of canine sins lumped together and called collectively the Jack Russell Terrier . . . whereas as rat killers they were excellent, they rushed in and slew foxes before they could bolt; they were so hard that they refused to give ground to a badger and were thus torn to pieces."

My Girl Friday

Mona Huxham, in *All About the Jack Russell Terrier*, tells of a representative of the breed named Cindy who fell down a mine shaft. All efforts to save her failed, her yipping grew weaker, and after much soul searching, Cindy's owners decided that, to prevent a slow, agonizing death by starvation, they'd best blow her up with dynamite. "This they did and her cries were heard no more." Soon after the owners got home, though, Cindy showed up at the door—"thinner and dirtier, but at least alive. The explosion had blown up the part where she had been imprisoned. She was able to dig through what was left and although she emerged in a totally different area from the one she had been in before, she found her way home in no time. These little terriers have an uncanny bump of direction."

How could any dog lover help but admire the breed? When Mrs. B. was pregnant with her first litter, I took up Donna's offer of a pup. I didn't really plan to hunt her, but I wanted a bitch in any event, figuring a female would be easier to handle than a male. Yeah, sure. . . .

🌿　🌿　🌿

Roz was eight weeks old when I brought her home from the Chesapeake, and weighed barely three pounds. She fit comfortably in the palm of my hand—so small that I worried, when I first showed her to Jake, he'd think I was offering him a snack. So I kept her in the car while I went in and prepared him for the great event. "I've got a new friend for you, Jake," I told him. "She's very young and very tiny, and you've got to take care of her, be nice to her, show her how to hunt—but don't get any romantic ideas." Just the thought of such progeny was chilling. Jake proved himself a gentleman.

By the time bird season opened, Roz was nearly four months old. She weighed about five or six pounds, her eyes barely cleared the tops of the mushrooms—much less the grass—but she was all heart. Russells are very companionable, indeed they hate to be left behind once they've been bonded, so remembering that Boomer had become a good bird dog, I took her out with us when Jake and I went hunting. What the hell, give it a shot.

At first Roz struggled along underfoot or behind me, yet she never complained. If she caught sight of Jake, quartering ahead of us, she ran to catch up. Even though Jake worked close, she was still too slow, too puppy-clumsy to keep up with the big Lab. But whenever she heard a grouse or woodcock flush, followed by the bang of the shotgun, her ears shot up and she leaped forward—"all atip," as the English say. As the season progressed, she ranged farther out from my footfalls. Late one afternoon, as we were sidehilling our way through some wicked doghair aspen, she was about five yards out from me and inadvertently stepped on a woodcock Jake had blown past. It sprang with a wild twitter from directly beneath her nose, she tried to leap for it, and I popped it at the top of its rise. But Jake got to the bird before Roz could. The light flashed on in her eyes—I've seen it many times, in mutts and in purebreds alike, in every kind of dog: the understanding that *this* is what it's all about, this is *hunting*. From that moment on, it was catch-as-catch-can.

They worked out a clever division of labor. Roz was mistress of the thick stuff. Cover that daunted Jake—and there wasn't much that could do it—was her delight. When she reached full size, weighing a bit more than twelve pounds, she was only ten inches high at the shoulder but twenty-five inches long from her upturned black nose to the tip of her docked, five-inch tail—almost a wiener dog in her proportions, ugly to look at but fun to watch. And fast. She could weasel her way into a tangle of blackberry briers or through the dense, matted blowdowns and undergrowth of the field edges like a tan-and-white flash of ground-lightning, putting out birds that Jake might have missed. I hung a bell on her collar to keep track of her whereabouts in those tangled thorn hells. Whenever she flushed a bird she'd yap angrily at its cowardice. "*Wimp, wimp, wimp!*" she seemed to say. "Why don't you stand your ground and duke it out?"

Then she discovered chipmunks and rabbits. She could dig like a badger, and when I missed the sound of her bell and went looking for her, I often located her from the tall, clattering rooster-tail of dirt her paws threw into the air like a nonstop mortar explosion—only her butt protruding from the hole, tail wagging madly. A Russell's tail provides a convenient handle whereby to pull it from the earth—like extracting a highly animated turnip.

Fortunately a little work with the police whistle eased that problem—two blasts would usually bring her pelting back, running side by side with Jake, but taking eight jumps to his one.

Then came the fateful day. I'd gone down to Joe Judge's place in October for the early duck season, and while I was there got to talking to a couple of other gunners—Jack Barry and Mark Masselink, whom I'd shot with before at Joe's. They mentioned they'd won a Ruffed Grouse Society raffle for a day's shooting at the Tinmouth Hunting Reserve, not far from where I live in Vermont. Did I know the place? Not only did I know it, I'd shot there many times, both the excellent sporting clays course and the stocked pheasants and quail. Tinmouth was first rate. They invited me to share the RGS largesse with them, and I did so gladly.

After a round of clays one frosty Friday morning in late October, we followed a guide named Mike Gallagher and his English setter, Remington, into Tinmouth's vast acreage of woods and overgrown meadows. The ringnecks held tight, as stocked pheasants will, but they proved strong fliers when we kicked them up. After we'd killed perhaps a dozen, Mike took us up to another field, stopping on the way at the clubhouse for a welcome cup of coffee. I'd brought Jake and Roz along with me that morning, keeping them in the Tinmouth kennel while we shot, but now I asked Mike if I could hunt them on our final swing. Sure, he said. Remington had worked hard and could use a break—let's do it.

It proved a mistake. My dogs were manic as hell, having spent the day locked in a kennel with the sound of gunfire echoing all around them—first from the round of sporting clays, then from the pheasant shoot not half a mile distant. They took off into a cornfield like a pair of canine Exocets, putting up half a dozen ringnecks well out of range. I whistled them back and gave them a sulfurous lecture, embarrassing them as much as they'd embarrassed me. They steadied down, and as we made our way from corn piece to overgrown meadow to woods' edge, Jake began to flush and retrieve birds as he'd been taught. Roz put a couple up, too, which we duly killed and Jake fetched. At the end of the far field, we turned right and began working slightly downhill. The field was studded with young white pines, branched clear down to the ground. My eyes were on Jake, working birdily back and forth ahead of me among some barberry bushes.

"Get ready!" I yelled to Jack and Mark. Jake blew two roosters out of the barberries simultaneously, the others shot, the birds tumbled in streamers of feathers . . . and out of the corner of my eye I saw a white-and-tan object disappearing like a snake into the ground-hugging branches of one of the pines.

Roz was onto a bird—one we'd already walked past, undetected by Jake—stalking it carefully, belly to the ground. Suddenly I saw the bird, a gorgeous cock pheasant, struggling vainly to get airborne, but unable to clear the low pine branches. I grabbed my police whistle to call Roz off—too late. She pounced like a panther. The pheasant was longer than she was, and nearly as heavy. But it was no contest. Her jaws closed on its head. Crunch. . . .

I bulled through the pine branches, grabbed Roz by the scruff of her neck with one hand, the pheasant with the other, and walked back out, up toward the others with my gun tucked under one arm. My face was burning.

"Hey, you got one too!" Jack was smiling. "I didn't even hear you shoot!"

"You don't want to know about it," I said grimly. I threw Roz's pheasant over to him. "Stick that bird in your game pocket. I'm taking Rozzie back to the kennel."

"Aw, hell, let her hunt on," Jack said, still unaware of what had transpired. "She's calmed down nicely now."

"You don't want to know about it," I said again, heading off toward the kennel.

We finished the afternoon in good order, banging more ringnecks and a few quail as well. I managed to redeem part of the day by making perhaps the longest successful wingshot of my life. A hen pheasant, one of the birds Jake and Roz had flushed wild at the start, got up between me and Jack Barry. I deferred to Barry's shot—he was, after all, the cohost of this expedition—but he didn't take it. When the hen was about forty yards out I swung on her without thinking and folded her with the first barrel. She had flown out over a low cliff, and fell beyond the rim. My Lab had marked her down, though, and went after her at a gallop. He too disappeared over the cliff edge, and my heart jumped into my throat. But I needn't have worried. Jake is as surefooted as a chamois, and by the time I got to the cliff he was already picking his way back up its sheer face, the hen dangling dead in his jolly jaws.

That night we all dined at the Dorset Inn, where Sissy Hicks, one of Vermont's finest chefs, braised some of our birds in white wine and wild mushrooms. I must have gotten Roz's pheasant. There wasn't a shot pellet in it.

Will I ever hunt Roz again?

Cold reason says no, yet I'm such a softie that I probably will. But only on grouse or woodcock, mind you—truly wild birds. Not on pen-raised pheasants, never again. They're not up to her style of hunting.

The Last Hunt

When my yellow Lab, Jake, turned 12 this past July, I decided the time had finally come to train a replacement. The breeder in Zeeland, Michigan, who had produced Jake for me fortunately had a newly born litter. I chose another male, who I named Bart—as in Black Bart the California stagecoach robber. The puppy arrived at our door in late September. He was a piece of work, all right—handsome, bright, so black that he went invisible at night when my wife and I took him out for a walk. Jake and our nine-year-old Jack Russell, Roz, were a bit put out at first at the arrival of this stranger on their hearthstone, but soon Jake adjusted to his presence. Roz still seemed a bit aloof, however, and indeed was off her feed. She was losing weight, and at first I attributed it to jealousy over the puppy's arrival. But the weight loss and lack of appetite continued, even after she learned to tolerate Bart, so we took her to the vet. There an ultrasound examination revealed possible cancer in her pancreas. Pancreatic cancer is extremely fast-moving. . . .

October 29, 2001
E-mail to my Wisconsin friend Tom Davis:

Dear Tom,

. . . Work with the new pup, Bart, is proceeding nicely. I'd forgotten how much time one has to put in on them. He's up every morning at 5:30, demanding to be fed (a real chow hound, like all Labs), then allowed to run and dump (how a big puppy like Bart can eat what seems so little and still produce such enormous poops totally befuddles me, yet he seems to grow an inch and gain a pound every day). He's seen plenty of birds killed over him—grouse, woodcock, pheasants—and loves to fetch them, though Jake usually dissuades him from that act of lèse-majesté. Bart inadvertently flushed a grouse yesterday, saw me shoot it, and seemed to see what it was all about. Nearly there. Two weeks left until the deer hunters invade the woods and I have to keep the dogs at home. . . .

It looks like my lovely little Jack Russell, Roz, only nine years old, has pancreatic cancer. Jack Russells normally live to 15 at least, sometimes 18 or even 20 years old. She's been a delight and a strange but wildly keen little bird dog, especially on woodcock. She won't eat, and I'm afraid I'll have to have her put down sometime soon. It will break my heart. . . .

C. SMITH '03

Robert F. Jones

I'm just back from a two-hour hunt with Roz in my favorite woodcock covert. I kept thinking of it as her last hunt. That's why I wanted to take her alone. But when we got in the truck, along with the gun, her bell collar, my shooting vest, boots, and all the proper gear, she acted disturbed, kept looking around for something. What she wanted was Jake. It was our time-honored custom. I went in and got him, leaving the puppy at home, and we headed out. The first hour produced nothing, though the dogs worked their hearts out.

A beautiful fall afternoon, most of the leaves gone, temps in the low 50s, blue skies with racing white clouds but just a light westerly breeze on the ground. We were at the bottom of the covert and turned for the truck. Just then Jake got birdy, moved into a hunk of puckerbrush and up popped Mr. Woodcock. I could have suspended my vow to spare these birds and killed it on the first rise. But this was Roz's hunt and I wanted it to be her flush. We marked the bird down, about 75 yards ahead of us.

We hunted back uphill, angling to the northeast, through dense briers and beggar's lice, doghair aspen and maple whips, low old crooked black apple trees that had laid a floor of miniature bowling balls for us to walk over. I called Jake to heel and hied Roz on ahead. She knows hand signals and followed my gesture into a thin stand of weeds. I could see her tail start to buzz and the bird got up, low, and I killed it with the first barrel. Jake broke away from me at the shot, but Roz got to the bird first. I called the Lab back, and for the first time in her life Roz had the delight of the retrieve. A male woodcock, as I'd surmised at the first flush. Then we went back to the truck and had a drink of water and a dog biscuit or two. They're quite yummy when you love your dogs as much as I do.

I hope it's not her last hunt, but if it was, it couldn't have gone better.

Best,

Bob

The Last Hunt

Tom Davis replied:

Hi, Bob—

I'm honored that you chose to share the story of what may have been Roz's last hunt. I can see it all, and I can feel what was in your heart. What a lovely way to remember her.

I'm not sure how relevant it is, but you'll recall that shortly before Timothy McVeigh's execution there was a lot of media attention focused on who was to be allowed to witness it. My wife and I were talking about it, and she said, "I just don't think I could watch. Do you?" My short answer was, "Yes," and I explained that after having held my beloved dogs in my arms as they've died, felt the last rippling tremors ebb from their muscles, heard the sighs as the final breaths left their lungs . . . well, compared to that, I didn't think I'd have much of a problem watching that coldhearted son-of-a-bitch check out. "Collateral damage," indeed.

You're clearly making the most of the time you and Roz have left—which, of course, is all you can do.

Best regards,

Tom

Next day I replied:

Tom,

Thanks for your thoughtful message. Here's some good news for a change. We took Roz to the vet this morning, where she received a shot of some magical elixir that has given her back her appetite, and she is once again eating—everything she can get her mouth around. The vet says she's feeling no pain from the cancer. I asked if it was time yet to put her down. The vet, a wonderful woman named Jean Ceglowski, looked shocked and said: "I'm not ready to do it yet. We'll keep her alive as long as we can keep her eating." Then she shook her head sadly. "Why do bad things always happen to the nicest dogs? I love this little girl. . . ."

Best,

Bob

But it was a short-lived hope.

E-mail to close friends:

November 5, 2001, a chill, grim, gray autumnal morning. Most of the fall color has blown, only a few yellow popple leaves flickering in the north wind. Up on the mountain, the red oaks glower.

This is a very sad day for us. We had to put Roz down this morning. The pancreatic cancer had moved into her liver. Last night she started shuddering and panting, her abdomen hot and distended. She couldn't even drink water. We gave her a Bufferin, then when that wore off, about 1 A.M., a quarter of a codeine pill. We were up with her most of the night; took her to the vet at 8 A.M. It was time. She went peacefully in about two minutes. We're having her cremated and will spread her ashes in her favorite woodcock covert and hang her collar and hunting bell in a tall, tall tree.

Both Jake and the puppy have been very quiet and know there's a change. They, especially Jake, will miss her for a while. We'll miss her forever.

Louise and Bob

Date: Monday, 5 November 2001, 08:38:23

From: John Holt

To: Robert Jones

Subject: Roz

Bob,

I'm terribly sorry to hear about Roz. In my heart, your home in Vermont and Roz are one and the same. She had enough personality to fill even a 10,000-square-foot house and was as good a dog as I've ever known. I can't think of what to say other than my heart goes out to both Louise and you. . . .

I'll think of Roz as I walk along the Yellowstone this morning.

John

Date: 6 November 2001
From: Dan Gerber

Dear Bob,

I'm so sorry to hear about Roz. It's the kind of thing you and I have both been through so many times, and it never gets easier, though it's a vital part of our relentless training in life and we have all those memories. As Rilke said, "but having been once, only once, it can never be cancelled." I came up with something a while back, thinking in that particular instance of my late wife, Virginia, and the thoughts and memories and love I still harbor for all the years we had together. "Love for the new is love for the old." I don't know if I came up with that or pulled it somewhere from memory. But it applies certainly with our dogs. My love for Willa [Jake's littermate] has been a continuation of the love I had for Lily [Dan's first yellow Lab]. In fact, I used to, and occasionally still do, call her Lilla—that abiding spirit through so many dog bodies. And I guess we too are abiding spirits through successions of bodies (beings). The energy carries on, finding new forms.

Love,

Dan

And that's the end of it. Rest in peace, my darling. . . .

MARK JEFFREY VOLK

Last Days

MARK JEFFREY VOLK writes with humor, passion, and insight into the sporting life of middle Appalachia. He fishes and hunts the streams and mountains of this beloved land. He writes about the people, the fish that have been caught and released, and the lives of his gun dogs.

He was raised in western Pennsylvania, and ran a timber company toiling alongside his workers. Once his daughter was grown and married, he moved out of the city to the Chestnut Ridge region. Mark Jeffrey Volk has written four books—*The Upland Way, The Hickory Wind, Homesick,* and *Pages From a Mountain Journal, Volume 1;* Volume II will be published during the summer of 2003.

It is from two of his books that the stories "Last Days" and "An Elegy for Dannyboy" were selected for the anthology. These pieces are used with the permis-

There was a time I lived by one of those calendar books you can buy in any drugstore. In it were appointed times, notes to remind me a check was due in or out, and myriad other things I dared not forget. But calendars, I noticed, can get to where they have too much say in your week and can come to run your whole life. I eventually had to put my foot down and figure out a way to live without one.

Abandoning that schedule book has simplified things, but sooner or later, we all need something printed to avoid missing the birthday of someone who matters, or for making sure we get to the dentist on the right day. It's best to know that you're not celebrating Christmas on the twenty-eighth of January. And that you're not hunting in a closed season.

But if I had my druthers, we'd mark the days by watching the seasons play out around us. It would be an almost perfect way to keep time and, if we pay attention, we just might see something new.

🌿　🌿　🌿

Calendars do have their place. For instance, a calendar will remind you which day is a last day. The last day before a fishing trip, the last day of bird season, the last day that camping permit for the state forest is valid. It's good to know which day is a last day, so we can prepare ourselves for it. Ironically, the only kind of last day a calendar won't remind you about is the kind of last day you never forget after it's passed. The last day's hunting with an old dog, the one you thought you were going to spend together last season but he just kept hanging on. Maybe it's the last day in a favorite covert before a condo developer runs all over it with a D9 Cat, putting it somewhere that you can't ever go to again.

Or it could be the last day that young dog acts like a pup in the woods and starts showing you what he's really got. Maybe last Saturday is the last time those brown trout in Sandy Creek will be able to fool you, because tomorrow's the day you finally figure out what they're taking. It could be the last day of a shooting slump that's been nagging you for weeks, or the last day before your son turns old enough to start hunting with you. Last days can be good just as often as not.

🌿　🌿　🌿

In 1980, I moved back to my hometown near the city after spending ten years living in the country. There were reasons for doing that which I felt were good at the time, but it left me in a vacuum in terms of familiar places to hunt and fish. I ended up driving the ninety miles back to the country for my outings each weekend, and, whenever I could get an odd hour through the week, learning what I could of my new home coverts and watersheds. It made for a lot of extra driving, but at least I was able to keep myself in hatches and birds during the transition.

I remember one of the trips back, a snowy day in 1983 that I spent in the thornapple bottoms of a place called Vickerman's Spring. Friends had warned me the birds were scarce around my old stomping grounds and that a trip back up would be a waste of time. But I felt I could find a few in some of my better, old covers. If any place could show me birds, it would be Vickerman's. When we left the van, there were big soft flakes falling that stuck to everything, and Dannyboy and I were soon soaked. It was the last day of the season and, as happens on that day, I was walking along feeling sorry for myself that I'd have to wait ten months until I could hunt again. I was also lamenting the fact that now it took almost two hours to reach this gorgeous covert that, for ten years, had been five minutes from my door.

There is a forty-foot-high wall along an old strip mine job that forms the eastern boundary of Vickerman's. Over the years, it's grown up into buffalo grass, red briers, and grapevines. I used to walk along the top of it while the dogs worked the edges and the steep grade down into the bottom, a strategy that put me in the clear if there was a point. Today it kept coming white with the swirling storm, and I could barely see down into cover. I stopped once to watch the snow falling from up there, and I remember thinking how far this was from where I lived now, both in miles and time. There were responsibilities waiting back in the city and, after gunning today, I'd have to head back. Come Monday morning, it would be the suit and tie, and the role, again. Them changes.

The silence roused me from my contemplation as if it were, itself, a loud noise, and I realized for the first time that I wasn't hearing Danny's bell. Looking in the direction where I'd last heard it, I spotted him pointing on the grade below. As I moved forward, a bird flushed and climbed steeply up over the top and sped down the path I was on. I missed it twice.

Following the bird's flight, we moved farther out along the hilltop and managed to start him two more times, each without points or shots. It's rare to get more than two or three reflushes, and I'd about given up on seeing him again, when the bell stopped one more time. I hurried toward the dog, who was standing rigid and proud, facing into a greenbriar patch that spread like a thorny spiderweb at the base of a white oak snag. The blowing snow stung my face and sprayed my glasses with melting drops, and my fingers were stiff from the cold and my snow-wet gloves. As I closed the distance to where Danny stood pointing, I heard a flutter on the far side of the snarl of vines and pulled down on a big rooster burning out the back like a gray-brown blur. My first barrel worked and he cartwheeled back down and hit the snow running, disappearing quickly into more briars.

Danny was the best retriever of all the dogs I've trained, and I wasn't worried about losing this wing-broken runner. Danny took off after it, he and my bird disappearing down over the slope, his bell fading away in the storm until all I could hear was the cold, wet hiss of the flakes as they settled around me. I knew my dog and I knew that I couldn't offer anything to the situation by following, so I sat down on a snow-covered rock, lit my pipe, and waited.

I had just gotten through the first few puffs when I made out the sound of his bell slowly working its way toward me. When Danny's white form emerged from the haze of hawthorn branches below me, he had my grouse, like I knew he would. As he delivered it up to me I saw the bird had a broken wing which explained the cartwheeling fall, but his legs were still sound, which explained the long, fast chase through the snow and brush. As I suspected, it was a grand big male with showy, bronze-tinted ruffs and tail band. Danny and I stood there drinking in the moment, celebrating this gift from one of our home coverts on that last day, and giving silent Thanks for some good years in that wonderful country.

🌾 🌾 🌾

Clair Adams was an institution in the town where I grew up. His name was a household word that inferred long, hard work and its subsequent success. Clair came up the hard way by growing his one farm and feed store into a regional chain during the thirties, forties, and fifties, despite the big Depression and WW II. But his exploits were past when I knew him in the late sixties. By then he was enjoying retirement, knocking around his original farm, raising a little grain for feed for his thirty or so cattle, and taking it easy.

Every hunting boyhood centers around a place like Clair's farm. From the time we were old enough, my pals and I spent uncountable days there, and Clair always made us feel welcome. Pleasant and laid-back, he was a man who had all he felt he deserved, and was satisfied with it. When we stopped to ask to hunt, he seemed happy to share a dab of his good fortune by allowing us to roam his woods and fields.

On muggy summer evenings as we sat watching his fields for groundhogs, he'd walk out from the big house and take a seat on the grass beside us. His were some stories; tales of droughts and prosperity, livestock epidemics and bumper crops, and how he and his family weathered the Great Depression. Our opinions and questions were important enough to him to take the time to answer, and he patiently listened and laughed at our boyish stories and corny jokes. I retain a memory of him as a gracious gentleman who enjoyed our company.

🌾 🌾 🌾

While I was living away from my hometown during the 1970s, there was a development boom that ate up the countryside where I'd spent my boyhood years. It changed the semi-rural world I had known in the '50s and '60s into a sprawling patchwork landscape of housing plans. I hardly knew the place when I moved back, and I found myself in a different hometown than I'd known before I'd left. The farms where I'd hunted were now suburban neighborhoods and strip malls, and the pheasants and rabbits were as gone as wild geese in December. The once-quiet back roads were now clogged with slow-moving traffic. Kids with profanity printed on their clothes, green hair, and nose rings gathered in front of stores built on hayfields that I had watched steam in the sweltering August sun. Our little village's downtown area became obsolete and deserted now that shoppers could find better parking and a much wider selection in the new shopping centers. I guess I was fortunate to get out when I did.

A theater was built where we used to pick raspberries as kids; but I remember one particular hot August morning about 1968. As we filled our pails, I took a step and felt something wiggle under my boot. It was another berry picker, this one black and white. I had blundered into his favorite spot and was just then standing on him, pinning him to the ground. But he still was able to wield his artillery and our relative positions left him with the ability to fire effectively and hit what he was aiming at. I got a real good dose. That was thirty-four years ago and I swear those canvas pants would still smell if I hadn't finally tired of the stench and burned them.

You can't really blame the old farmers for selling out after years of living as they had, working hard in all kinds of weather, bearing a burden few would tolerate for long. It would be more than I could resist if a developer called with the offer of a check with more zeros on the end of it than I'd ever seen. Visions of a Florida retirement can dance around in a sunburned mind when it's old and tired. No worries of rain, warm all year long; such bait would get you, too. Clair held out for three years after the boom started, then leased the farm to an agribusiness conglomerate and moved south. The outsiders came in quickly, took over everything, and posted it all. They cut and burned the hedgerows and berry patches, and grew crops by clean farming, eliminating the fencerows where the hen pheasants and rabbits hid their young. I stayed away from Clair's place and kept busy working, and saved my outings for weekends in other places. I didn't want to look at it anymore than I had to, and, when I drove past the old farm, it was like an unknown place.

Finally, Clair's was sold to be the site for several hundred plan homes, and I decided to go back for one last hunt. My journal notes for that late November day in 1985 tell that it was a cold Saturday morning about nine-thirty when I left for the farm. I parked at the end of the old lane back to what had been our groundhog hunting field. As I turned Danny loose and started up through it, I thought about the old hunters who used to come here and wondered where they'd gone.

In the old days, small game hunting was part of the weave of our community. I knew the Bennet brothers, Frank Shuster, the Nicoletts and Murrays, the Stouffers, gunners from my boyhood. Those men could be found there every week on those long ago November Saturdays, as if they were observing some national holiday. In those days, hunters stopped to chat when they met in the fields and woods. Guns were pointed down and actions opened as they smoked and talked. Most of us were neighbors, and conversations centered around family and school, work and home. Information was shared about how the season was going. There was the obligatory speculation as to where the pheasants and rabbits might be found. Youngsters were welcomed, teased, and wished good luck, and old-timers were accorded an appropriate amount of deference. After talking, smokes would be snuffed out and intended directions settled on so that no one felt crowded. Guns were reloaded as everyone walked away, the slide sounds and clatter of the Ithaca and Winchester pumps coming back as shells were stuffed into magazines. But all that was now long past, and the men I'd known from those other years were not hunting the hills of Clair's farm now. I wouldn't trade memories of any of it for anything.

Coming back to myself, I started toward the chicken house woods.

Last Days

Danny and I headed for the thicket and hunted it through, jumping a couple rabbits but no pheasants. There were pink surveyor ribbons on short stakes scattered throughout the field, and I could see where the streets were to be laid out, with a cul-de-sac on the hilltop. The spring was still there on top, and under the trees, its clear water bubbled up out of the ground rocks like it always had, finding the light of day as it emptied into the trough where Clair's cattle used to loaf. Our beagles had found refuge in the shade there years ago, too. Soon, strangers would only find it a convenient place to turn around, and all those days spent in this place will belong to the ages. I stood, looking and remembering, while the breeze stirred in the dried, brown goldenrod. Danny cast in and stared impatiently at me, wishing, I'm sure, that I would snap out of my ruminations and catch up. I did, and followed after him.

🌿 🌿 🌿

We hunted out across the hilltop to the woodlot where my pal Bobby had shot a big fox squirrel the year before we started our senior year of high school. The woodlot was gone. Someone had cut the big hickory trees that once stood there and bulldozed them into a muddy slurry of roots, branches, and dirt. A knot took form in my stomach and I turned away. Danny cut over in that direction and suddenly stopped on point at the far end of one of those piles. I headed for him and stopped a few yards short of where he stood. There was a cackling eruption from the tangle, and a big ringneck pheasant climbed up into the airspace above it and seemed to hang there, trying to make up his mind which way to go. I miss plenty of grouse, but to me a pheasant's flight seems like the ponderous travel of a hot-air balloon. I pushed the barrels up and through and fired. The bird hesitated, his wingbeats stuttered to a stop, and he up-ended and slipped back down. Danny ran in and had him and carried him to me, sitting to deliver like he thought he needed to remind me what a prince he was. I can't remember ever shooting a ringneck that big, and we sat there for long minutes, admiring him. In a distance, the drone came to me from the earth-moving equipment working over in the hollow where we ran our schoolboy traplines. But, right then, my world was exactly that ringneck, my setter, and this old place. Time, for a moment, ceased to move forward, and we reveled there in what had been, and was now coming back, now that I'd come home. The only thing that could have made it any better would have been to look up and see Clair coming toward me through the goldenrod, wanting to sit and talk.

🌿 🌿 🌿

An aged or terminally ill gun dog should be allowed what time he can handle in coverts for as many days as he can. It's kinder to allow him that than to restrict his final days to sleeping by the fire and trips to the vet. Let him work at his own pace. You'll know when he's had enough and needs to go home, and, in the meantime, you'll witness something you won't forget. There are few things more heroic than a dog doing his best to hunt in the face of old age or an affliction that's robbing him of his strength and vitality.

During Danny's last woodcock season, I tried with every resource at my disposal to find him a flight of those birds. Woodcock can be charity for a dog going down, an easy hunt on flat terrain with birds that hold well under a point. But the flights were thin that season, and it was the tenth of November when a friend found a few birds. He knew my situation and called with the tip. This was going to be a day just for Danny and me, so I left young Hunter at home.

The covert we gunned that day is typical Allegheny woodcock country, flat, open bottomland with hawthorns, gray dogwood, alders, and a slow-moving stream. I hadn't hunted it in a couple of seasons and was unsure what to expect, but that day it shone. There was a pair of birds that lifted when we made our first cast, and we began moving others right after that. But there were no points at first. Finally I heard the bell stop and hurried to where it sounded last. There is a series of beaver dams in this place, and the shallow backwaters cover acres of ground. It was along the far side of one of these still pools that I found him, pointing under hawthorn trees. I moved around to a more open position, and, when the woodcock came up, it dropped at the shot. Then another flushed from the same spot. I passed it and sent Danny in for the retrieve. He searched and found and brought me the bird, then was off again.

Within five minutes he was pointing again. This time the bird got up concealed by alders, and I didn't get a chance to shoot. But there were more as we continued upstream. We had a nice two-and-a-half-hour hunt, during which I missed three and made a shot on another. There seemed to be woodcock everywhere that day. All it took was to push a little farther, although many went up hidden or flushed too far. Danny overheated quickly in the humid, sixty-degree air, so I took it slow, letting him rest as he needed through the lazy, low-pressure afternoon. With the stream close by, he had plenty to drink, and I carried along a few snacks which I gave him at intervals. He repaid me well, with plenty of action and eleven good strong points.

Finally, at the far end of the last pass, we reached the fence on the next farm. Here we would have to start back. Danny was beginning to show fatigue again, and I didn't want to wear him down too much. I decided to cross the creek on the footbridge and head us straight to the truck. But, on the far side, he pushed into more alders and worked the new piece like a pup. In less than two minutes, the bell was silent. I hesitated, moved forward a few more steps, then listened.

Over his life, Danny had developed the habit of stopping to listen if he lost track of me. When he did, the resulting silence of his bell would sometimes trick me into thinking he was pointing. I would whistle, and, if he had been trying to locate me, he'd move after hearing it, letting me know he was hunting again, and off we'd go. But this time, as had happened many times before, there was no answering bell when I whistled. I felt he must be on point, and looked for him for close to ten minutes without finding a trace. Then suddenly, his bell sounded in front of me. I found him standing in hardhack, looking like he'd found something he wanted me to see, so I started toward him. He saw me coming and turned and headed off into the brush, where his bell went silent again. I'm sure he'd been pointing and, when I was unable to find him, he came to get me. I found him locked up solid, but in a sitting position, loyal enough to hold my bird for me, but too tired to remain standing any longer while he did it. Yes, I did my part when the flush came and yes, he did his by retrieving the bird to hand. And yes, there was a tear in my eye.

That seemed to be all he needed that day, and he followed me back to the truck at heel, tired, but very pleased with himself. I had to help him up into his box in the truck, and he was asleep before I started for home.

🌿 🌿 🌿

The last day of the 1994–95 shooting season was great, a contrast to most of the days out up to then for that year. The early woodcock shooting was very thin. That unhappy state was followed by the warmest, windiest, early November in my memory. Conditions like that play the devil with dog work, and Hickory and Hunter performed poorly. Then, on the tenth of November, I was subpoenaed to testify for a family I had bought timber from the year before. They were being sued by a neighbor over a right-of-way, and I had hired a surveyor before I cut their timber so I knew the property lines.

I hate being in court. Attorneys are seldom interested in what really occurred, and make you feel like you're on trial, even if you're only a witness. My stress levels go through the top of my head, and I usually end up telling somebody off. Those proceedings were dragged on for several months, and I lost most of the only nice days that fall because I was sitting in court assisting in a matter that really had nothing to do with me or the timber I had bought. My landowners eventually won their case in late winter, partly on the strength of my surveyor's testimony. The family's attorney was profuse with his thanks, and he assured me I'd be paid for my time. But three years later, the check still hasn't come. Who would have thought? It's probably just lost in the mail.

I did have two good days over Thanksgiving (court was closed), but the bad weather returned after that and there were only a handful of huntable days in the late season. One was a grand day on the eastern slope of Laurel Ridge, where a warm sun on two inches of snow that was breaking up nicely gave me a day that stood out like a pearl in a skillet of sawdust.

My first stop was a hollow I should have ignored. The hawthorns there are wonderful October covert, but, by late in the season, it's devoid of birds, as it was that day. I drove to another place nearby, an abandoned farm that was timbered in 1983. It's grown back to perfect cover. What isn't grapevines and succession forest is slopes and gullies carpeted with greenbriar, which, that season, were loaded with berries. Grouse tracks were everywhere in those ravines, and the dogs and I were into them from the time we left the car to our return at sundown. I was shooting my twelve gauge L.C. Smith and holding out for shots over points. In the two and a half hours we were there, we moved nine birds for fourteen flushes, with eight points. We left seven grouse there and drove back to town into a beautiful winter sunset, unaware that we'd just spent what would turn out to be Hickory's first good day into birds and Hunter's last.

I don't know about you, but numbers like that are plenty good enough for me. Go ahead and take those road trips to a far away country. Whether my days have lots of bird contacts or just a few, I always feel better hunting around home.

☙ ☙ ☙

For the next two weeks, what didn't fall on us, blew past. Add to that the fact that I found myself in one of those slumps gunners have to learn to expect from time to time. The chances just wouldn't come, or, if they did, the bird went out in line with one of the dogs. Shells mis-fired, points were empty, and, behind it all, there was that nagging lawsuit that stole more days than I was willing to part with.

The last two days of gunning were as much a contrast to each other as that day with all those grouse at the bottom of Laurel Ridge was to the rest of the season. Friday found me on a mountainside above Apple Creek, trudging through six inches of snow and feeling every degree of a minus-twenty-five windchill. I was hunting Hickory alone, and he jumped a deer which he pursued, with great vigor and speed, out across the slope. When I pushed the button on the training collar transmitter hanging from my belt, he seemed indifferent and contin-ued merrily with his pursuit. I got him back about an hour later and found that the collar was missing. All that remained was the trans-mitter. It would be three weeks and almost four hundred dollars before I was able to replace the collar, too late for that season and that day; troubles with bird dogs.

By the time four-thirty arrived, I hadn't seen a point or a chance worth mentioning, and, Hickory, delighted with his new discovery of the sport of whitetail chasing, chased deer most of the afternoon. I was cold and weary from too much of every way a season can go bad, and I found the path out and headed for the Jeep.

Saturday came up warmer and, after reminding myself that this was not only a new day but the last day until October, I headed for Larry's farm on Chestnut Ridge. Larry is one of those people who always seem glad to see you. I've never stopped to let him know I'm going to hunt that he hasn't invited me in for something to eat. You insult him if you don't at least have one cup of coffee.

I think Larry and his wife are foster parents. I don't know for sure and never felt it was my business to ask, but I've never seen some of the children they keep there, more than once. The racket gets to me if I stay too long. The littlest ones show me their crayon drawings from school, and they started calling me Uncle Mark on one visit. His wife is seldom there when I am, so I don't know much about her. Larry says she "works at the hospital." It's hard to stay less than an hour, but I feel I should be polite considering how hospitable they are. When you walk back outside, you feel like you were just visiting family.

One day I ran into a hunter I knew who was coming out of cover next to Larry's property. He mentioned that he had gone as far as Larry's line, then turned back after all those stories he'd heard about Larry and his lunatic wife shooting at each other and anyone else who dared come up to the house to ask permission to hunt.

They's crazy, said Martin. *He just got out of prison for armed robbery and I ain't goin' up there anymore. He told us to not even bother asking to hunt cuz he'd run us off the place, if we survived the gunshot wounds.*

Martin, I've sat in his kitchen and had breakfast with the man. He was fine. The kids are clean and seem well behaved. Are you sure we're talking about the same guy? I asked.

Don't mention them kids to me. They broke into Harvey's barn, let the cows out, and tried to set it afire, he replied. *That whole crowd down his place is nuthin' but criminals an' no'accounts. They just got you fooled, that's all.*

Well, he lets me hunt, always asks about my family, and tells me to stop sometime when I can stay for supper. You can't ask for a nicer guy than that, I countered.

They got ya fooled, you'll see. Someday you'll come out of the woods an' yer Jeep'll be burning and your dogs'll be shot. They's that kind, I'm tellin' ya.

Hill people can have a peculiar way of seeing things, and it takes years for opinions to either change or become further set. Maybe Martin or his people had a run-in with Larry, and Martin's decided it's his business to trash him and his family in the local gossip mill. I've seen it happen a lot up here, and the outlandish stories some of them tell on each other defy probability. Still, it's part of the local color and, if you plan to spend much time around locals in these parts, you learn not to take much of what they say about each other too seriously.

I stopped to tell Larry I was there that Last Day, but no one answered the door. Maybe they were out pulling a bank heist or a serial killing, I can't say. But I can say that the grapevines in the first hollow got the day started right.

As I walked down into the woods, Hunter worked into a tangle, and a grouse flushed out the back, followed by another one seconds after the first. I whistled my setter in and we moved on down the path, hoping for a reflush from that pair. When we came to the boulders along the run, Hunter stopped for a drink. I waited for him to finish and listened to the sound of the tiny stream as it spilled down over the mountainside. We hadn't gone another twenty-five yards when we bumped a grouse that came up over me. I started to mount my gun then decided not to shoot without a point. The afternoon was just starting and there was still time.

About twelve years ago, I started to rethink my shooting philosophy. It was in response to unintentionally shooting a pair of yearling grouse on a late November day. The dogs and I had just left the truck and entered a nice hillside covert I'd found the previous season. After about thirty minutes, both dogs got busy near a ravine and pointed. I got two good chances on two that came up almost together and in the confusion, I shot both of them, something I never do. As the dogs went in after the shots, more grouse started coming out of the same tangle until a total of seven had flushed. All of them were very close to me and slow enough to see very clearly. There was one large bird that looked like a hen. The others were mixed males and females, all of them smallish. Two landed in trees after flying just a few yards and sat there looking at me like fool hens. The others seemed to land just a short distance across a clearing. Although it was late November, this was obviously a brood, still together and unmolested enough to be unsure of what threat I might pose.

Last Days

When Danny and Hunter both returned with their grouse, I examined the birds. Both were yearlings, a hen and a rooster. About then I realized I'd just killed a brother and sister, and that I felt awful about it. Angry with myself for shooting both on the same flush, I went home and didn't hunt for two weeks. Those two birds weren't the first yearlings I've shot, nor were they the last, but they changed twenty years of gunning attitude in me.

As a result, I made some new rules for myself, and now stay within the bounds of that code between the dog, the bird, and me. Although I don't look down on those who do it differently, it's my way of addressing what I was feeling about the killing component of upland shooting. For me, the sole purpose of an outing never has been to kill a grouse. It isn't for most gunners who have any heart. I've simply added some conditions that need to be met before I pull a trigger.

It became my goal to try to orchestrate an encounter between the dogs and the bird. If the two of them do everything just right, I will take the shot. There are no shots unless over a point. If it's a woodcock, I shoot no more than two a day, and they must be over a solid point, not flushed if the dog breaks. If I'm hunting with a friend, one person goes in for the point, not two. This way, if the bird exploits the terrain, wind, or conditions to its own advantage, and the dog's unable to pin him fairly, he's safe. The grouse wins far more often than I do, and that pleases me. I usually manage to stick to these self-imposed rules. On those occasions when I give in and don't, and there are a few every season, I feel bad for days about my cheating.

Maybe I'm making too much of all this, but I don't think so. Thoughtful gunners have been refining their ethics for generations, and, to some degree or another, we all try to stack the deck in the quarry's favor, even if it's only refusing to shoot a bird while it's sitting in a tree. After all, that gun in our hands gives us a mighty big advantage over the wild things we seek.

Which is why I passed that bumped bird.

As we worked out the hollow, I was rewarded for the shot I hadn't taken with a nice point by Hunter. When the grouse flushed from the far side of a brush-covered log, I missed the first barrel, pushed the gun ahead and tried the second, which worked good enough. Hunter made a nice retrieve (aren't they all nice?), and delivered up a mature male with black ruffs, a grand gift from Larry and his covert.

That was enough. I pulled the two smoking empties from the barrels and didn't replace them. Instead, I walked along a skid road and let Hunter work the remaining country ahead of us. I had started late and knew he wasn't up to a full day's hunt, still we pushed farther into that hollow on that last afternoon. There were more grouse in there, and he gave me two staunch points, and enjoyed himself thoroughly. When we reached the end of the last cast, I turned down what I thought was the right tote road out, and walked it back up the hollow, my old setter following behind, tired but happy.

At quarter to five, with the dark settling quickly, I realized I still wasn't near the truck; instead, we were at the far end of the main hollow. Unsure which of the tributaries would bring me back out at the spring below the farmhouse and my Jeep, I paused to try to figure out just where I was. If I took the wrong branch, I'd find myself on the ridge below Larry's, which would require that I retrace my steps and try another ravine. If I tried to cut up over the top and down into the next little valley, I'd get tangled up in the almost rim-to-rim laurel thicket there. I knew it would take two hours to crawl through it in broad daylight. Now that it was almost dark, I'd stand little chance fighting it. I probably wasn't going to die, but if I misjudged, I'd be out there till nine or ten at night, and my family back home would be worried. As I stood there wondering which path to take, Hunter seemed to sense my concern and started down what I was sure wasn't the right path. He went about fifteen steps, turned, and looked at me like he was saying, *It's this way, dummy, trust me. Dogs are good at this.* Since I wasn't sure either, and didn't have any better ideas, I obediently followed along. After a couple hundred yards, the surroundings started to become familiar again in the failing light, and, when we stepped up out of the woods, the truck was just where I left it. Satisfied with himself, Hunter sat down in front of me with an expression that was priceless. He had showed me where the birds were hiding, why couldn't he find a big truck?

The cancer that would take him from me a month later was growing in him even then, though I didn't know it at the time. He had become disoriented several times that day and seemed run down. But, in spite of that, he had come through one more time at the end of that afternoon and got me out and back to the truck when I wasn't able to do it on my own.

I put him in his box in the back, turned and looked west. The last of the Last Day sunset glowed while the thinnest shaving of a moon hung suspended in the cold sky. In another minute my dog was snoring, dreaming, I hope, of that last point and that last retrieve, the last he would make in his eleven years under my gun. The mountain had been kind once again.

🌾 🌾 🌾

I buried him a month after that day, up on Larry's Farm. I called Larry from the vet's and, when I showed up at his place, he motioned to me through the kitchen window, pointing to the tote road that heads down into the hollow. I gathered up the blanket-wrapped body of my dog as Larry's oldest boy came out of the house carrying a pick. He reached into my Jeep and picked up my shovel, and together we walked the path down into the hollow, never speaking.

We stopped at the boulders along the run where Hunter paused for that drink on his last good day, where he bumped that grouse I passed. I laid him in his blanket on the snow and, together, Larry's boy and I dug a grave for him. Afterward, I marked the place with a small pile of stones, then we headed back. Larry was watching from the window as I stowed the shovel in the truck. His son walked over to the porch, stopped at the top of the three steps, and turned to me.

I'm real sorry 'bout your dog, sir. I just had to bury one of ours, so I know how you feel. I'll keep my eye on his grave for you, just to make sure nothing bothers it, okay?

It was the first he'd spoken.

Yes, I'll appreciate that. Thanks for helping me, I said.

As I drove out the dirt lane to the highway, I slowed and looked one more time at the hollow. The boy was still standing on the porch and saw me stop. He waved then turned and walked inside and closed the door. I haven't been back to Larry's place, but it's not because I'm afraid of the lunatics the neighbors say live there.

🌿 🌿 🌿

Last Days can bring a gift of another sort; by then my reflexes are as quick as they get. My dog and I are never in as good of shape as we are on the last day. The dog's ribs show through the hide on his flanks like pickets on an old fence, and the muscles in his legs and mine are harder and tougher from the hills we've climbed. We are, by then, a complete contrast to the condition we were in before things started in October. Lazy summers play the devil with one's physical condition, but I usually manage to lose about fifteen pounds by the last day. It's ballast that will find its way back on again if I'm not careful. While good music and a good book can build the mind, they soften a back-side, and can undo a person over time.

At that final dusk, when all the days of the season are spent and gone, the woods behind us feel a little empty. Now the wilderness gets the time it needs to rest and replenish itself. Soon, the warmth and green-ery that comes back with the spring will hide and nurture the young ones that come in early summer, and the whole thing goes on and on.

🌿 🌿 🌿

All gunners have Last Day rituals, and they should be faithfully observed every year. At home that night, the guns are cleaned for the last time a little more thoroughly. The pockets of our jackets and vests are emptied of twigs and weed seeds. Shells are put back into their boxes, unfulfilled hope in red plastic bundles that now must wait till next year. Leashes and collars are gathered, and boots are cleaned and dressed. All of this reminds us the season's gone till October. Already we miss it and look forward to Fall.

Back when I was more gregarious than I am now, I would host a big game dinner for my friends, where we'd toast out the season in front of a roaring fire. This year, I'll do the same, but it will be just Hickory and me. After, I'll sit down with my journal and tally points, birds moved, hours spent, and days enjoyed. These numbers are not for charting "scores," but for determining my dog's progress and the scarcity or abundance of grouse in my coverts. When I'm done with the arithmetic, I can see weak spots in the dog's work that I can concentrate on in the yard training before next fall, and I'll know which covers are down and maybe should be left alone for a season or two.

When I get to the summary page for the year, I compress the months of things observed and lessons learned into a synopsis that's always very illuminating. Patterns emerge that weren't clear until the Last Day. Sloppy dog work under certain weather conditions is noted and remembered for future reference. Maybe I'm having trouble with flights at a certain angle. Practice with the hand trap might help.

Some years, chance and a season will toy with me. As they see fit to do so, the weather, the points, and the woodcock flights will veer off their usual course onto some strange tangent and end up giving me either diamonds or stones in abundance. While I'm in the middle of all of it, I'm unable to figure out what it's trying to say. Then, on that Last Day, I see the big picture clearly for the first time. If I've spent the season doing things with the right attitude, I will have usually been blessed by the mountain. But if I was too anxious for a shot, if I didn't spend enough time appreciating the sunsets, if I wasn't as patient with the dog as I could have been, or was too preoccupied with things that had nothing to do with shooting, the mountain might have run out of patience and given me a couple of good smacks. Wrong attitudes have a way of coming back around and getting us, and some years you won't see the whole picture until the Last Day.

🌿   🌿   🌿

Hopefully, none of us will know when we've spent our last days in our favorite places. The last point we'll ever see will seem like all the rest at the moment we see it. We hear the clock ticking for our dogs, our seasons, and ourselves, every day, but the last tick we hear will sound like all the ones we heard before as we try to squeeze all the living we can out of every minute and every season. I want to spend my last day on a vine-shrouded mountainside, listening for a bell that sounds somewhere up ahead, and hoping to hear it go silent. And I don't have to say that I hope I won't know which one will be the last one I get to hear. Thinking that our Last Day is still far off, and that there will always be another season to be lived, helps us stay a little ahead of the curve when those last days come around, as they always do.

MARK JEFFREY VOLK

An Elegy
for Dannyboy

There's a heavy oak dresser at the foot of my bed—rescued from a burned out building—I bought to renovate during my working life in the city. My wife at that time and I stripped and refinished it, replacing the scorched and rusted hardware with polished brass pulls and cornices. It's a gorgeous piece and I'm very proud of the grain and character of the wood we brought back to life under the new, rubbed oil finish we applied. Sitting atop the dresser is a carved, scrimshaw likeness of a black-and-white setter, given to me by that same wife several months after the death of my black-and-white setter, Dannyboy. It was a sweet gesture on her part. She knew what he meant to me and, the summer after he died, she found this carving at a yard sale and brought it home. I'm not superstitious, but on the bottom of the statue is the inscription: *Carved by Charles Parrish on 1/20/89.* That was the same day Dannyboy died.

And there have been other things, peculiar events that I can't explain. For instance, there was the October day I took Hickory, while still a youngster of two, up to the site where I buried Danny. I wanted him to see the spot where one of his predecessors slept away the autumn afternoons. As we climbed the last hill to the grave, Hickory became strangely animated, as if he sensed we were setting about something important. As I sat by the pile of stones I had placed as a marker, he danced and yelped and carried on like a puppy. How could he have known?

Or what about the way the gunning always seems better than average if I hunt on an anniversary of his death? Just last year, ten years to the day after Danny's passing, I had a marvelous afternoon in a new covert, with birds aplenty and several good chances over nice points. It was the best day, in terms of weather, that I'd seen for weeks, and Hickory and I came home that afternoon flushed with the fullness of a successful day.

There have been times I thought I heard Dannyboy barking late at night; and other times when it seemed Hunter or Hickory was backing another setter on a point, only I couldn't quite make out the dog in front. Gunning friends still talk about hunts we had over him, and how he seemed to make birds appear from nowhere. Was he a magical dog? I guess that depends on your definition of magic. He was to me.

❧　❧　❧

On October 20, 1977, a privately chartered airplane went down near Gillsburg, Mississippi, killing the flight crew and three members of the band Lynnrd Skynnrd. Only coincidentally, that was the day Dannyboy was born. I had just turned 25, and was playing in a local rock-and-roll outfit that covered a lot of Southern Boogie and Blues, so I felt a kinship with those musicians from Gainesville, Florida. Something went out of me when the news of their plane crash came over the TV, and I bring this up only to give you a sense of the time and place that was when Dannyboy came into my life.

He was descended from pure field trial stock, big-going dogs with no natural retrieving bred into them, but lots of drive and focus. He was one of a litter of eight; five males, three females. When he was four weeks old, I went to see the litter; we knew we belonged together as soon as we laid eyes on each other. After that, the parents' owner, a game warden and hunting buddy of mine, swore Dannyboy waited for me whenever I wasn't around. The night he was nine weeks old, I drove my 1967 Plymouth through an appalling blizzard to pick him up and bring him home.

🌿 🌿 🌿

There are many good training systems for starting a gun-dog puppy, but I decided to follow just one. We started with the "noise at mealtime" drill to condition him slowly to the point that he'd not be gunshy. I also taught him his name and to come when called. And, of course, I had him pointing a grouse wing on a line until he tired of that at 15 weeks. He graduated to training quail and more demanding drills in the space of five months, absorbing his lessons like a sponge. My journal records that I was impressed with his intelligence and very proud. By the end of his first year, Dannyboy had grown into a loyal, powerful little fireball that weighed in at about 55 pounds and lived to make me happy. There were the usual kinks that still had to be worked out between us: his range, staunchness, handling. And I had to learn new ways to control all that fire he carried into the woods. But, through all of his ups and downs, his promise remained obvious, and I knew it was only a matter of patience and working it out; time would bring it all together.

Time was one thing we had plenty of, day after wonderful day, living in the center of miles of good country. We hunted the corn and wheat fields for September doves, Danny's first go at retrieving. There were the big swamps and swales of October where the flight woodcock stopped over. There were still a few native pheasants in the long, narrow cornfields of early November. And through the season, from autumn's bright, heavy leaf cover to January's frozen white mantle, there were grouse. The two of us learned from each other as we went, by trial and error, and by just digging in and doing, always following the outline in the training book I reread constantly from cover to cover.

I've written before of our first outing on woodcock that first October, how it rained hard and how we hunted anyway. I was working days and playing the clubs and parties at night, so I took any chances to be out, despite the weather. Danny and I fell into a pattern of going and, those first couple seasons, my journals record that we hunted rain or shine or blizzard.

🌾   🌾   🌾

Planted, preserve pheasants sit tight and provide a controlled situation that can be arranged specifically to benefit a young dog and I recommend them without reservation. There was a small commercial shooting grounds about 12 miles from my home, where a pheasant could be released, shot over their or your dog's point, and then dressed out, tagged, and packaged for the princely sum of $7.50. I took Dannyboy over there every time I had an extra few bucks.

Once, I had a neighbor along to take pictures. It's strange to see an image of yourself walking in on a point, then shooting, and, finally, accepting the bird from your dog, all from the visual perspective of a second person. I have some of the best of those pictures framed above me as I write this. Dannyboy and I will be forever young in those photographs. It's hard to believe we ever looked that way.

His second season, 1979, was one I'll always treasure. That year, October came on deliciously slow as summer faded across the countryside; change, barely moving from tree to tree. The air chilled a little more each late afternoon and evening, cooling the woods and the rivers a few degrees each day. The lessening sunlight and cold nights kindled flames in the treetops everywhere you looked, each week's brilliance sweeping you along, touching your every nerve and fiber, getting a little closer to the bone every evening.

That was the season Danny showed me just how fearless he was, whether facing thick briars or a farmer's bull. If either threatened to interfere with our gunning, he dove in with sincerity and nerve, refusing to allow anything to keep us from our quest. Twice that year I had to pull him out of greenbrier tangles where he enmeshed himself so badly that, every time he moved, the thorns cut him deeper.

There was a bull that grazed with the herd on the Jonas Place, who was of the strong opinion that his pasture was private property. Once, while Danny and I were crossing the pasture, we came over a small rise and found ourselves facing the bull at close range. Sensing we had no quick escape, the old boy starting advancing on us, one step at a time. Danny put himself between me and the surly bovine and stopped, holding his ground. The bull stopped, too, and the two of them proceeded to stare each other down, the bull flapping his ears and stomping with a heavy front hoof, Danny growling. Suddenly he barked sharply two times, and advanced, showing his teeth. The bull's eyes bugged out and he backed up, turned and trotted away with a frustrated snort. It may have just been my imagination, but it seemed to me he wasn't sure whether this man in red and his sawed-off companion were a threat or not, but he wasn't sticking around to find out. Danny looked back at me with a triumphant grin, then darted off toward the edge cover to resume his search for woodcock.

🌾 🌾 🌾

Each season, peculiarly, one or two birds stand out for me from all the others. Perhaps it's a particular point in a certain place or a certain afternoon, or a particularly well-handled situation by the dog or dogs. I can't say for sure what makes those chances float to the top among the couple hundred other flushes we have over a three- or four-month season, but, each year, those one or two encounters distill the year down to just a couple of very significant moments. I don't always make the shot, though sometimes I do.

I remember one such incident that last season before I moved back to the city. It was warm and rainy, late October day and the remnants of Indian summer's bright leaves still hung in the trees, their colors now dimmed like a watercolor painting, distant faded splashes of color streaked with the black of wet tree trunks. I parked at a gate that led back to a grown-out country cemetery, and swung Danny into nine-bark and hawthorn thickets that grew along the path. Above us, a redtail, up high on those humid thermals that lifted from the hills below, screamed twice then tilted off for parts unknown, annoyed with my setter and me for interfering with his hunting.

I soon found splashings of woodcock sign, and, shortly, Danny was locked up. I missed clean, both barrels. One nice thing about woodcock shooting, if there is only one, is that there are usually several birds nearby. I had a nice two hours there; with eight good points, but only two more chances. Once again, I missed both. So far, it had been a good day for the birds and Dannyboy, but a poor one for my shooting skill.

Around 3:30, I heard Danny's bell go silent and found him along a tiny run, afloat with fallen thornapples and a flotilla of bright leaves drifting downstream toward the village like little yellow sailboats. It was a good, high point on a grouse. It flushed just on the other side of the canopy and gave me only a glimpse and time enough for one quick chance, but that was enough. The little double spoke its awful death and the bird cartwheeled down. Danny sprinted after the wounded runner, finally returning with it ten minutes later. Retrieving: that magnificent violence we train our dogs to do because our senses, and sensibilities, don't allow us to carry out that task ourselves.

We sat there and admired the big hen with black ruffs as her bright eyes faded in death. She was the grouse that came to mean that season to me, shot in cover atypical for that wonderful country; lowlands, slow moving streams under hawthorn thickets and the quiet of farm country. She was the last grouse I shot in the Igert Farm Covert.

🌿 🌿 🌿

When I want to objectively determine the actual truth about how a dog is doing, I compare his points to his bird encounters. In other words, of the total number of grouse flushes we have in a given period, how many of that total did he point. If we move eight separate grouse with eleven flushes, the number of productives is weighed against the *flush* count because each flush presents a new opportunity for a point. Danny was my best, with a lifetime average of 37 percent of flushes pointed. Hickory, my current dog, is second with an overall average of 29 percent in seven seasons. That's better than one point for every three birds flushed for Dannyboy; and a ratio for Hickory of better than one point for every four. If you know much about gunning grouse in the Appalachians, these are fairly respectable numbers, and more a reflection of the dogs' natural ability than my training talent.

Here, I'll mention two things about training gun dogs. As I said at the beginning of this piece, Danny was not a natural retriever. He came into it, both from a desire to please me once he knew what I wanted, and as a result of his natural instinct to get to the bird. Most setters will, to some degree, want to pick up a fallen gamebird. Where it gets hairy is what happens immediately after they pick it up. I'm convinced that the field trial stocks we have today, dogs with the retrieving bred out of them to intensify their pointing instinct, experience a measure of confusion as to whether they're actually supposed to touch the bird. Add to this confusion the tendency of most gunners to say *something* to the dog, either congratulatory or scolding, the moment he grabs the bird. This adds to the bewilderment in the dog's mind. Because of this, the dog will usually either bite down and run off with the bird, or cringe and drop it.

How you react to his behavior at this point will go a long way toward determining what kind of retriever you end up with. Danny was too focused to drop any bird he'd pointed, I'd shot, and he'd found. His reaction was to bite down and refuse to relinquish it. I ended up with some pretty chewed-on gamebirds the first two seasons. Over time, we worked it out through consistency, patience, and that water bottle trick I mentioned in *The Upland Way*.

🌱 🌱 🌱

Generally, he was a dog who lived to make me happy. But early on, Danny had a problem with range, and we had some moments over that. Knowing what I know now, an electronic training collar would have helped. The collar enables you to consistently reach out and touch a dog wherever he is at the precise moment he does what he knows he shouldn't. The collar I use these days has worked wonders with Hickory, a strong-headed dog who constantly pushed me to the edge of absolute frustration during his first couple seasons. There were days he simply didn't care about what I wanted, and had to be controlled mostly by fear of the consequences of his misbehavior. By allowing the person in control to react immediately to a dog's pushing out too far, or any other infraction of his training regimen, a collar used correctly usually doesn't take long to solve obedience problems. That is, *if* the user did his homework in the first place and remains consistent with his actions.

These problems are part and parcel of a gun dog's early training, and, if you're going to shape a dog into what you want, you've got to be willing to pay the price of hard work, lots of time and structured, repetitive practice; waiting it out till you've built that pattern of obedience. A dog's manners can make or break a day afield, regardless of how much time you've spent finding a special covert, or equipping yourself with only the best. Life's too short to dance with a partner who steps on your feet, or shoot over a dog who doesn't obey. I won't do either, and neither should you.

ꕥ　ꕥ　ꕥ

Dannyboy and I had to endure the transition from life in the country to life in the suburbs when I moved us back to Pittsburgh in 1980. Not being able to hunt every afternoon after work was a big adjustment. The reasons for returning made sense to me at the time, but there were times for years after that when I pondered the wisdom of that move. Why is it that the mature, responsible thing to do seldom places us where we want to be?

An Elegy for Dannyboy

I buried myself in my new business, and Danny spent the days out in his kennel run, no doubt wondering what *we* were doing there amid all those houses, noisy streets, and people. There were lots of backyard dogs in that section of town, and, to the neighbors, I'm sure Dannyboy was just one more. They had no way of knowing the kinship he and I shared when we were in our element, how he became an extension of me out there, and gave me gunning days I'll always remember.

🌿 🌿 🌿

I used to hunt with companions more often than I do now. But, over the last six or eight seasons, I've found myself becoming more and more of a loner when the shooting season comes around. To me, hunting with a partner is a little like kissing your significant other in front of a crowd. Physically, it's possible, but it's much better, and more enjoyable, if no one's looking.

I spent the weekends scouting new coverts in the mountains east of the city. Paladin Run belonged to a doctor I knew and was one of the best I found. It was nestled in a deep hollow, along a feeder creek just above the base of the east slope of Big Laurel Mountain, back a long, brushed-in lane. For some reason, I only ever hunted it alone, maybe because it was a small covert, or because it was one of the first spots that was kind to Danny and me in our new country. I never wanted to share it. The owner told me he'd bought it in the mid-1960s as an investment and, right away, had sold the timber. In 1980, when he gave me permission to gun there, it was perfect, albeit steep, regrowth cover.

Danny and I would come in from the top and hunt the skid roads across the face of the hillside, gradually working down to the creek bottom. Then we'd work up the opposite face, ending at the top where we'd take another path the long way around and back to the car. I can't say if anyone else ever hunted it, we never saw anyone, but the birds acted like we were the only people they ever came in contact with.

The best day Danny and I had there was on December 27, 1981. I had moved five separate birds on the way down the first hillside, none of them giving us a point or a shot, although Dannyboy was trying hard. As we swung past a small stand of open pole timber, he pointed along the edge of it, but the grouse flushed low, stayed in line with him, and I passed the shot. Along the creek, I decided to follow another skid road that ran downstream along the waterway. After about a couple hundred yards, I heard the bell go silent and moved toward Danny. One by one, three grouse lifted. The last gave me a lovely chance, quartering away left, that I missed twice. None of the first five had come this way so these had to be new birds. I followed the one I missed into a short ravine choked with redbriars and hardhack. Suddenly, Danny was pointing again and this time I made the shot when the bird lifted and headed straight back up the mountainside. Danny found it, dead, a yearling hen, but didn't retrieve.

Continuing downstream, now more relaxed with a grouse in the vest, I let Danny work the cover on the slopes above me. Grouse started flushing every hundred yards, or so it seemed; some over points, some were bumped. Because most appeared to fly downstream, the same direction we were headed, it wasn't possible to accurately count how many were new birds, but it didn't matter. I unloaded my gun so I was free to watch Danny work all those grouse, and he did me proud.

As we approached the mouth of Paladin Run, where it joined the bigger stream near the summer cottages, I turned us back up the nearer mountainside on another skid road and soon got a nice point into a laurel patch. I reloaded and walked in, but the bird flew out, sound only, and I lowered the gun. Just then there was another flush at the site of the first, and a grouse rose in front of me, hanging for a split second over the thick greenery of the laurel. I fired the first barrel and missed, calmed down, pulled back onto the bird with the second barrel and touched off, which did the job. This grouse was brought in with style and laid in my hand; one of the first full retrieves Danny pulled off. I made a big fuss over him. I think that was the day he began to get the idea that I wanted him to bring *all* our birds to hand, although it took another full season to convince him to consistently retrieve that way.

Spending all week waiting for Saturdays only served to intensify Dannyboy's need to be hunting, and he took full advantage when the weekends finally came. He was a thinker who worked until he had it figured out, and over the next few years, he developed that wonderful bird sense that only comes with time in and miles covered. One of my older friends, a long-time dog man, made the comment once that Danny's head was never in the clouds, but down there among the details, down in the tangled heart of things. During that period I watched him come of age in those mountains east of the city where we lived.

There's a depth to a specialist you won't find in a jack-of-all-trades. Focus seems odd to those who only skim the surface of life's passions. The man and dog who hunt for a little of everything, everywhere, usually don't attain the deeper understanding of those who live, eat, breathe one or two gamebirds in a finite setting. Dannyboy was a dog who made the most of focus we lived with and, because of that, became the standard by which I've judged other peoples' bird dogs. He had bad days, as any of us, or our dogs, do. But, in the larger scheme of things, his way of meticulously covering the thickets we hunted, his brilliant handling of grouse and woodcock, and his tenacity when it came to searching for wounded game, made him the best of a couple of pretty impressive setters I've had the pleasure of following into cover.

      🌿   🌿   🌿

I killed my 100th grouse over one of Danny's points. It was the first day of the fall season in 1985. He and I had gone to Chapel Creek hoping for woodcock, but there were none in. I decided to hunt the dense thorn thickets on the hill above the stream, and we spent an hour in there, moving grouse that were only flush sounds through the dense hawthorns.

Chapel Creek is a vast bottomland, but it can get crowded on a weekend opener. When I heard several close shots, I swung us back down to the water. There, I sat along the edge of the creek and watched Danny wade out and settle down into the cool water. He spent a full minute submerged to his neck before wading out and shaking, spraying me with muddy water. Then he laid down beside the log where I sat and sighed with satisfaction. I sat back against the tree behind me and drowsed, watching the oily reflection of the sky in the smooth surface of Chapel Creek through half-closed eyes.

My reverie was interrupted when another shot rang out from just downstream, and I heard a dog whistle then someone shouting. Despite the vastness of the country I was in the middle of, my location just wasn't safe with other hunters that close and unaware of me. I headed us off through the bottom at right angles to where the noise seemed to be coming from. Another shot from that direction brought a hen grouse sailing over, but I held fire; it didn't seem right to ambush her as she was fleeing someone else.

Changing course again, we headed east toward the base of the mountain and worked our way out through nice low alders and red brush cover. Danny bumped another grouse a short time later; it landed in front of me and ran into a tangle of alders, then reflushed out the back.

Near the car, I stepped out of the cover into a wide field and almost gasped at the panorama before me; the enormous valley blazing with purple asters and saffron-crowned goldenrod, woods edged with bright yellow and orange and red leaves, a blue haze partially screening the far mountainside, and the vast silence of it all.

Danny came running in and slammed, suddenly, onto a point next to the field. I hurried over and walked into a tight-sitting grouse that flushed low over the open ground and tumbled at the shot. He brought this one, also, and laid it at my feet. I wasn't aware of it at the moment, but, later, when I was filling out my diary, I discovered it was number 100 in my log of grouse taken up to that point in a lifetime of hunting.

☙ ☙ ☙

Gunning the bigger mountains southeast of home one late December afternoon with Storm, Dannyboy's litter sister, and her owner, John Carson, confirmed the reason for George Evan's admonition not to hunt young dogs of similar age together. They played and ran and wrestled for the first two hours out, and we walked and talked, catching up on family news, ignoring the dogs. I didn't always stay as alert as I should have in those days when I had a friend along; if I had it to do all over again, I'd have paid more attention. It's a mistake I made, one I can't call back, other than to take care not to repeat it. That day seemed to set a pattern, and we had little success hunting Danny and Storm together for the rest of their careers.

☙ ☙ ☙

Hunter came along during Danny's eighth year, a dog who seemed ardently happy from the time I brought him home at nine weeks, until the cold, late February morning in 1996 when my vet and I eased him into eternity. In spite of his relaxed, low-key attitude. Hunter understood his job more than he ever let on, but, rather than let it consume him much, like Danny did, Hunter made it part of a larger, fun picture. As a result, I was constantly surprised and delighted by his ability to handle grouse, probably the toughest gamebird for a pointing dog to manage, and the way he learned to back Dannyboy on points. The result was two seasons of brace work I still daydream about.

Dannyboy and Hunter were setters with very different styles and temperaments. Danny was patriarchal and, from the very beginning, made it plain to his younger kennelmate that he was boss, the alpha dog; even though Hunter outweighed him by 20 pounds and was 30 percent larger than Danny. It was seniority determined by age rather than size and strength. At times, they'd argue, mostly while in the kennel, but it only took a snarl from Danny to put Hunter in his place. As a result, Hunter became the most docile dog I've ever owned, completely subordinate to me and to Danny, who strutted around Hunter like royalty bent on constantly reminding his subjects just who he was.

Hunter was a natural clown; teasing and nagging Danny, often to the point of frustration. Dannyboy retaliated by never backing Hunter on any points that I can recall. Hunter, however, backed Danny anytime he found him locked up. There were instances when I still don't think Hunter actually saw Danny pointing, usually due to heavy cover between them, but, somehow, sensed what was happening and stopped and froze stylishly.

But if grouse were a challenge for those two, the gentle, tight-sitting woodcock were child's play. It was in the bottomland hawthorn and alder thickets that they made the most of the fall flights, and gave me brace work on woodcock that raised the hair on the back of my neck and still does. Someday, I may tell you about it.

But it was a double point they gave me on a grouse on the spine of Laurel Ridge that keeps coming back to mind. It was a breezy, late January afternoon, and very cold. We'd hunted for four hours and hadn't found a track or heard a flush in what had been a cover where we moved seven for nine flushes in a three-hour hunt one day two months before. We hadn't hurt a one, and I had hopes for this later day.

Coming to a small hollow filled with grape tangles, Hunter finally stopped on point, but the grouse got out screened from view and headed down the ravine. I took the moment to sit down; the dogs came in and, tired themselves, laid down in the snow. I remember how the bare branches nodded in the frigid wind above me and how the gray clouds smudged the sky as I tried to keep from shivering, but failed miserably; it was just plain uncomfortable to be out. I kept thinking about how warm it was at home. In winter, sometimes it's the coming back to a sweet, warm house that's the best part of a day's hunt.

An Elegy for Dannyboy

For some reason that afternoon, an article came to mind that I'd read in a gun-dog magazine just the week before. The story was written by a man who's been writing for as long as I can remember, and, to my knowledge, has a loyal following. He told, in great detail, about executing his dog after learning it was terminally ill; coming home sad from the vet's office, getting a shovel and his .357 from the house, walking the old dog at heel out to the backyard, digging a hole next to the garden, and commanding the dog to sit down in it. You can imagine the rest. The story tried to read as sentimental, but I've seen what a large-caliber round does up close, so the point he was attempting to make never came through. It was a brutal and barbaric story, and I was both shocked that he wrote it and the magazine printed it. Steaming, I sent a letter to the publisher offering to lend that writer the scratch he'd need to have a veterinarian do the job the next time. As I sat there looking at those two wonderful setters asleep in the snow, Hunter's foot over Danny's back in a gesture of affection, I couldn't imagine ever being in a state of mind where it would make sense to shoot either of them.

As the day grew late, and I grew colder, I roused myself and the dogs and started a meandering trek back to the road. As we came to yet another small ravine, I heard Danny's falcon bells go silent first, then Hunter's louder cowbell went still. I moved in and found them locked up close and high headed, the older dog's tail just three feet from the younger dog's face; both so intense they seemed about to catch fire. The image of the two of them, an orange Belton and a blue one, back dropped against that wall of laurel, bright green in the late afternoon glow, would have made a magazine cover. The grouse came up, the gun fired as if by itself, and the bird dropped. It was over in just seconds, but became a memory that's lasted for years, as much for that grouse as for that superb double point.

This time, with his competition along, Danny brought the bird to hand; then sat and grinned at me like he knew he'd done the right thing. You'll never convince me that a bird dog doesn't understand, even when he acts like he doesn't. Maybe the trick is to get him to love you enough to put the icing on the cake whenever it's *the* perfect time to do so.

🌿　🌿　🌿

We had those two good seasons of brace work, and I watched the two dogs develop into an honest pair, a team; Danny working the fringes and Hunter staying in that crucial middle ground between me and the older dog. Someday I intend to go through my journals and count the double points they gave me. I remember feeling, a few times, that, with them, I had an unfair advantage.

🌿　🌿　🌿

As a gun dog ages, you find ways to favor him in his final seasons. As much as I loved to see the two of them working in harmony, I knew I had to give Danny a few hunts without Hunter on some of those last days out. Hunter hated that, and told me so by bugling like a coon dog when he saw me open the kennel gate on Saturday mornings and let only Danny out.

On just such a day, in November 1988, I took Danny, solo, to a great little hollow of slashing and vines that belonged to a man named Daryl, a customer of mine. Daryl owned the local diner and didn't hunt anything but deer, but had promised me there were plenty of grouse on his land. In exchange for a "deal" on some product, he gave me permission to hunt there. But my hopes for the day were dashed when I found another vehicle along the main road fronting his ground. I went in anyway but soon heard shooting ahead. I turned us in a new direction and hunted the fringes to avoid the shouting and gunfire that was now coming from the center of the woods.

That day, it became obvious that Dannyboy was slowing down. His casts were shorter and not as quick, and he came in more often to check with me. The terrain in Daryl's Hollow pitches almost straight up, then back down, unable to make up its mind, unsure of where it wants to go. Danny had a rough time of it there, though it seemed that he hoped I wouldn't notice. There's something very brave about an aging dog hunting what could well be his last season. The old sparks are fading and, although the fire still burns, if you look close you sense the smolder beginning. You hate to see it, but there's a richness now that's come from seasons spent together. The memories are as much a part of each day out as the day itself. That day, I'd brought some extra energy snacks for Danny, and he gobbled them with great relish. For a while, they seemed to give him a lift; but then he seemed to wilt again. More than once that afternoon it occurred to me I should have taken him to a gentler covert. There was no mistaking the signs, I was seeing the final season in the life of a grand gun dog.

When it comes, this realization is filled with mixed emotions. You notice more keenly your old dog's ways. There's a nagging sadness; every little event that would be just another element of a season's ritual now becomes so significant, so special. Colors burn deeper, sunsets fix themselves in your mind in ways they hadn't before. It's, at once, an extraordinarily bittersweet yet triumphant time you never forget; you find yourself intensely happy to have given you both the shared days. I can't think of a single experience in life that's quite the same.

We never had a point or a chance that day in Daryl's Hollow. After that, I began working him only after Hunter had been taken back up. Giving him the last 45 minutes was as much to allow Danny the chance to still feel needed, as it was for me to avoid admitting he was having his last season.

A trip to the vet prior to the season's opening had revealed nothing to be alarmed about, other than age. Shortly after that hunt at Daryl's, however, my journal records that I began noticing a redness and irritation in Danny's eyes. I assumed it was some kind of allergic reaction and took him back to the vet, who prescribed an ointment that didn't work. When the condition didn't clear up I took him to another vet who diagnosed it as another kind of allergy and prescribed another ointment that didn't work. What followed was a nightmare of bad diagnoses and ineffective treatment. Danny, it seemed, had everything from stomach ulcers to iron-poor blood. About that time, his appetite started to diminish, so I took him to yet another vet, who smelled as much of hard liquor as of the pets he spent the day treating. With a wave of his hand he announced that Danny had hemorrhoids and pink eye, but there was nothing he could do for either.

A week later, I found what appeared to be a tumor growing out of the corner of his left eye. It was really nasty looking and resembled a piece of raw steak turned on its edge. Having gone through all the vets near home, I was desperate and began networking among other gunners I knew with well-cared-for dogs. Finally, I got a recommendation, from a customer who raised pointers, to try his vet at the other end of the city.

The waiting room was crowded as I sat nervously till our turn was called. Dannyboy was clearly uncomfortable and wouldn't lie still for long. I walked him into the examining room, and put him on the table. The doctor came in, took one look at him from across the room, and let go with a resigned sigh. After checking and re-checking Danny closer, the vet turned to me with a grave expression on his face. It was a tumor, probably malignant, and he should operate the next morning to determine the extent of it. I needed to leave Danny there so he could be sedated until then because he was in pain. The doctor didn't offer much hope.

My head was spinning as I drove back to my office. That night, as I tried, unsuccessfully, to get some sleep, I kept seeing him pointing grouse. At 9:30 the next morning, the call came.

It's time to let him go, Mark; the tumors in his head and throat will strangle him within a couple of days. Like a voice at the end of a tunnel, I heard myself tell him to do what had to be done, then added that I was on my way. Outside my office, the January air was clear and bright and sharp, but it was all lost on me. At the vet's I wrapped Dannyboy's still warm body in his old green blanket and loaded him into the back of my van, then drove home to pick up Hunter, a shovel, and my gear and gun. We were in the middle of a city, not where Danny and I belonged at that moment and it suddenly made sense to be in the mountains.

I buried Dannyboy with his bell and collar in a covert that had been a favorite of his and mine. Then I stepped back, fired two shots over the grave from the doublegun he served, said a short tribute in a private gesture of affection and parting, and felt absolutely awful. Hunter sat nearby, an orange Belton mourner, atypically somber and quiet.

There was a fire burning in Dannyboy that only dying was able to quench. When I buried him on that January morning, I left a piece of me in that grave. Hardly a day goes by that I don't think of the time we had as we grew into what we became in the upland shooting equation.

🌿 🌿 🌿

Emotionally, the first time you lose a dog is the worst. While your world doesn't end that day, a small part of it changes forever. Afterward, you feel different about the death you bring to the game. At least I did, because now you're even more aware of the measure of stillness dying brings.

Go through the loss a few more times over the seasons, as other dogs pass through your shooting days, and you begin to see the whole process in yet another way. There's an old Celtic song about life's *recurring* tragedies, and how, over time, you grow numb. The chorus wonders if we just get stronger or more used to the pain, a question I cannot answer. It's not that you're any less shaken when it happens after the first time, it's just that now you realize loving dogs and letting go of them is part of the whole; no less tragic, but one more element of the cycle we become part of when we decide to hunt wild creatures over dogs. When they leave us, whether in our arms, or on the cold steel of an operating table, the same old pain and sorrow come back around, only this time, the pain is reprogrammed by the repetition. I remember how bad I felt when I realized this, how I felt I wasn't doing honor to their memory. But it's an inescapable reality, and you've got to accept it. Proceeding through a succession of gun-dog lives is like living through a series of shooting seasons; they become a celebration, an observance of hunting's ritual, and poetry and art, what others have called a rare privilege. But the training, growth, attainment, elation, and the aging of a gun dog, come as part of one whole package, one that ends in loss. You can't have a little bit without accepting it all.

🌿 🌿 🌿

Upland readers permit their writers to wax sentimental over the aging and loss of a gun dog. But when you lose something that meant the world to you, and was important enough to write about, you can get trapped in stringing together some pretty syrupy words that sound like every other story of that ilk and mean nothing special to anyone but you. A dear old dog deserves better than that, and I decided to wait this ten years in hopes of avoiding the tempting, hyperbole-laced words that would have come had I written this story any sooner. The memory of a dog who touched you inside and changed you forever merits a special dignity after he's gone. There's a sort of pride that should go along with his life and death that needs time and reflection to fully grasp and then articulate. I owed Dannyboy this story, but it needed to be written with the reverence I've tried to infuse here. He rated that from me. Besides, Time isn't really an issue if a gunner is fortunate enough to have recorded the story of his friend in pages that, hopefully, will be reread and understood long after the both of you are gone. Are such dogs as you and I gun over worthy of any less?

DAVID WEBB

Among
the Aspens

DAVID WEBB was born in Indiana, raised in Ohio, and lived in Illinois before settling in western Pennsylvania with his wife, Emma. He received a BS degree from Baldwin-Wallace College in Ohio and a Master of Forestry from Duke University in 1963. He spent thirty-five years in the professional field of wood coatings and wood preservation, and published over 40 technical articles in those areas.

A longtime target shooter, Dave has written many articles for *The American Rifleman, Handloader,* and *Rifle* magazines, and contributed pieces to the *Gun Digest* and *Handloader's Digest.* His focus on upland birds and Brittanys led him to write stories for *The Ruffed Grouse Society* magazine, and Dave recently edited an anthology

I reflect on the faint whisper of the autumn breeze. It comes mixed with the turning of the aspen leaves to golden yellow. I stop, listen, and watch the pieces of gold as they dance with the slightest whisper of wind.

Several times a year I visit this little grove of quaking aspens. There are eight or ten trees still standing where once there was twice that number. Twenty years ago a bulldozer cleared an adjacent woodlot area for a small housing development. The windbreak was lost to the aspen covert, and over the next few years many of the trees were uprooted.

entitled *A Feisty Little Pointing Dog — A Celebration of the Brittany,* published by Down East Books.

He has bred, trained, field-trialed, shown, and hunted Brittanys for going on thirty-five years. He and Emma are now "empty-nesters," with their three sons pursuing their own careers. However, each has a Brittany of his own, and their youngest son is actively involved in field trials.

There are currently three Brittanys — Dewey, Cocobean, and Herb — in the Webb household.

There are several new aspens in the grove that have sprouted or germinated from seed. The buds of the young trees provide a rich nutrient source for grouse. Here in western Pennsylvania aspens tend to not be as long-lived compared to the majestic northern red oaks.

My tranquil walk through the aspens is often when the golden yellow shower of leaves is falling to the ground from the overhead branches. I like to hear the leaves rustle in the breeze and the soft sound as each leaf lands on the covert's floor. I'll stand motionless and gently move the golden yellow pieces with my boot.

🌿 🌿 🌿

I reverie about an orange-and-white Brittany that moved quickly through those golden leaves, and then whirled on point. The grouse appeared to be pinned. The dog with his head and short stub tail held high. Rocky was gathering in the scent to locate the bird. His feet never moved, as he seemed to lean into and then back slightly from the grouse scent. The point was solid.

Taking several steps, I moved past the motionless Brittany and then the wings of thunder erupted. There was no twelve-gauge double in hand to follow the bird's flight, as it was two weeks before the opening day of grouse season. At fifteen months Rocky was not steady to wing. His pursuit of the bird was not much beyond the aspen covert.

Within a minute or two he was back at my side. I talked to him

softly, telling him "what a good pup he was." I rubbed his ears, stroked his back and ribs—

The trance was broken as several golden leaves bounced from my uplifted face. I stood near the hallowed ground, beneath which the Brittany had been placed, wrapped in his blanket with his collar still in place. He could have undoubtedly had many years in our grouse and woodcock coverts. I then looked down and stared at the aspen leaves. They became cloudy as I reflected on the Brittany's first grouse point among the aspens.

DAVID WEBB

Coco Lives Forever

It is entirely possible to be mesmerized by a puppy's stare. Just ask my wife, Emma. We were selecting as a Christmas gift a Brittany pup for our second son, Dan. There were nine pups from which to choose; at eight weeks old, three were liver and white, and the remaining six were orange and white—all females.

Em was elbowing me. "That pup in the corner over there is the one we should get for Dan. Look at how she just sits there, watching us."

The little liver-and-white pup—as most all of them are—was adorable. She would look at us and cock her almost solid liver-colored head from side to side, while her littermates were scrambling and jumping for our attention.

The pup never did get involved in the fracas. She just sat there watching us. Coco did not go home with us on that occasion, because as I told Em, Dan would want an orange-and-white Brittany. So we chose a leggy, ear-licking pup, who was given at Em's suggestion the name of *Buon Natale*—meaning "Good Christmas" in Italian. Dan's new female pup would have the call name of Tally.

As the Christmas season passed and the New Year entered, Dan would in the next several days be returning with his new pup to his place in the St. Louis area. I had a short two-night business trip to make. On the first night out when I called home, Em regretfully told me that my 14-year-old male Brittany, Manny, who had been ailing for the past couple of months, had died during the night. Dan had found the dog in the morning and buried him near a small group of sassafras trees.

I reflected on the fall season of the year—the color of those sassafras leaves would have been similar to the orange of that Brittany. The leaves rustle and fall from the trees, a grouse flushes as I walk the nearby wooded hillside, pondering the empty collars of several Brittanys that my three boys and I had been fortunate to own in our pursuit of upland birds.

The next day I returned home from the trip. Upon entering the front door, Dan and his mother greeted me; both looked most definitely like they had something to hide.

They did.

My youngest son, Joe, came out of the kitchen holding that little liver-and-white female Brittany, whom we named Coco. If ever there was a pup that took me hostage, she was it. She lavished her affection, and I was absorbed with the thrill of it. Over the next several months that special bond developed. She followed my every movement. Where I went in the house, she followed—from room to room. We thought of renaming her Shadow.

Even though we had owned Brittanys since the early 1970s, Coco was the first to be allowed in our home. She had the usual number of accidents that any young pup will have during housebreaking. But she learned quickly, and soon her daily activity and routine fit into our schedule.

A somewhat unique situation for Coco was a rather unfortunate one for me. Within the month of the pup's arrival in our home, I was diagnosed with a detached retina in my left eye. Following the surgical operation and a two-day stay in the hospital, it was going to be necessary to recuperate for an additional ten days at home. The doctor had prescribed rest, with a strict set of instructions for limited activity. Of course I never mentioned the new pup in the house.

Coco was unbelievable. She seemed to sense a need to be more restrained. This was a puppy just four months of age, who was limiting her activity. As I recuperated she was my constant companion.

As the spring weather arrived there were numerous forays into the nearby fields and woods. As Coco matured it became apparent that she was different from the other Brittanys we had had. Oh, how she could run.

She did not always listen and come when called. There were times she would be gone for twenty minutes to half an hour, but always ahead out in front, hunting. When Coco was eleven months old her desire for running and hunting became intolerable for me. It was becoming almost uncontrollable. It was almost as if she were Jekyll and Hyde—the wild thing, and then the quiet, calm, well-mannered pup that would lay at my feet by the fireplace.

It was a difficult decision to take Coco out of our home and deliver her to Dick Keenan for some field and obedience training. Dick and his wife Esther were the Brittany breeders from whom we had originally obtained the littermates, Coco and Tally, Dan's pup. Although semi-retired from the training of pointing dogs, Dick had indicated a willingness to work with Coco.

As I drove away from the Keenans there was a sense of guilt on my part for leaving Coco behind. She would be there for a month; it would be possible to monitor her progress. Dick had asked that I wait for ten days before returning to see Coco's progress. On that day I had alerted Dick to my approximated arrival time. He and Coco were waiting.

"Before you renew your acquaintance with your pup, she has a thing or two to show you about finding birds," Dick said, telling me that he had released ten quail. As we walked to the field he gave the command, allowing Coco to start looking for birds. She raced out across the field to the far edge and quickly proceeded to point, jump-in, flush, and chase the quail. She located all ten and then some as she followed-up several birds for a second find.

As he snapped the lead on Coco, Dick remarked, "I think you have yourself a nice little bird dog." We exchanged comments about the pup's bird-finding ability, her pointing style, and most important, her snappy run. Oh, how quick she was!

"Have you ever given consideration to entering a dog in a field trial stakes?" Dick's question sort of took me by surprise. I never really had, but with Coco's run maybe it just might be fun to see what she could do.

Upon returning home with Coco, she made me literally pay for the four weeks she was with the Keenans. She sulked! In the family room, she would go to her corner next to the fireplace and just stay there,

paying no attention to my wife or me. It was undoubtedly her way of getting even with us. But all seemed to be forgiven after several days, and she was back to her old self.

The next several weeks were spent as often as possible in field training and conditioning Coco in preparation for the trial. She most definitely had the endurance—more than enough for the 15- to 20-minute run that was the allotted time for an Open Puppy Stake in an AKC field event.

After her somewhat limited field training, I hoped that Coco was ready for the puppy stake. Dan had agreed to accompany me to the AKC Brittany trial, which was being held in the northeastern part of Pennsylvania, almost three hundred miles from where we live. It was going to be a somewhat long weekend trip. Dan did not plan to enter his pup. There just hadn't been sufficient time for him to give Tally the field-conditioning work that was necessary for her to run.

Coco ran the race with reckless abandon. When the announcements were made for the Open Puppy placements, Magic Magnum's Coco had been selected for the blue ribbon. There was indeed great joy in Muddville—even though it was not a baseball game.

The long drive home was pleasant. Dan and I talked about our two Brittany littermates and reminisced about our hunts together, birds missed, and all sorts of good times afield.

Early the next morning I departed on a business trip. En route from the airport a call was made to Dick Keenan to tell him of Coco's win. The euphoria was brief. I returned home to a grave loss.

It is as clear in my mind's eye as if it happened yesterday. I can see her silhouette hanging in the kennel. Her collar had gotten caught in the opening above the door. I flung open the door and grabbed Coco. My first thought was to breathe life back into her. She was gone. A terrible accident! The "what-ifs" were constantly being asked for days, weeks, and months. Even now some years later I ponder the loss.

Coco will live forever in my thoughts. She will always have a special place in my heart. As Ben Hur Lampman suggested, that will be Coco's final resting place. She had two points toward a field championship—the blue ribbon placed on the den wall is a constant reminder of her former presence in our home.

Coco . . . Oh, how she tore at the heart. As Rudyard Kipling wrote, a pup will give "love unflinching that cannot lie." The dog has a magical power over those who are willing to give unselfish devotion. A dog has devotion that does not waver. Coco will live forever!

BILL TARRANT

Ol' Drum

The late **BILL TARRANT** wrote a bird dog column in *Field & Stream* magazine for over 20 years. This monthly column probably earned him his rightful place as America's favorite gun dog writer. He authored eight books on gun dogs and their training. He won numerous awards, including the Outdoor Writers Association of America's prestigious Deepwoods Award, and was twice named dog writer of the year by the Dog Writers Association of America. He was an active hunter and trainer, and competed in field trials with his gun dogs.

With permission from his wife, Dee Tarrant, two of his stories are included in this anthology: "Of Miracles and Memories" and "Ol' Drum."

*I*n the early 1960s there were three zany waterfowlers who hunted Cheyenne Bottoms next to Hoisington, Kansas. There was Doctor Robert Moore, the vest-pocket-sized dynamo who was an All-navy boxing champion and ate roasting ears the way computer printers throw a line on a page. With him was Jim Culbertson, who'd moved to Hoisington to coach the high-school football team, the Cardinals. Doc was the team physician. And last was this writer, whom the two of them permitted to tag along as ballast.

Probably the most novel lodging I ever had while hunting ducks was that year I checked into Doc's hospital for a thorough physical examination. My camo and waders hung from the room's wardrobe rail. The nurses would awaken and feed me before dawn, and up the curved *drive, coming in his International Scout (with a shotgun hole in the floor-board) and dragging a monstrous airboat, would be Doc. Doc had all the gadgets. Even a duck-plucking machine in a small room from which he would emerge looking tarred and feathered.*

In the evening I'd be released to join Jim, and the two of us would go to Doc's house for a duck dinner—cooked by Doc's wife Bea—and poetry. Doc loved heroic poetry; he had a lot of Charles Kuralt in him. It was the finest of all arrangements.

Well, Doc was a thoughtful sort, and he had Senator Vest's speech printed up about Ol' Drum, the hound, and gave everyone a framed copy. Mine hung over my typing table for thirty years. Then one day something prompted me to look up, push back, stand, and head for Missouri to write Ol' Drum's story.

Here it is.

🌿 🌿 🌿

Turn the clock back 122 years, bare your senses, and attend to this scene. The Civil War has been over four years. Nowhere has it left deeper scars and a more granite temperament than in western Missouri (they said, "Show me!") where two armies and assorted renegade irregulars had pillaged the countryside and terrified the people. Every Missourian knew of death and destruction, so his response had become quick to fight, to be self-sufficient, to forever hold a grudge, to be inflexible in his opinions, and demanding of justice.

Now, narrow your focus. It is rolling country, heavily treed, with intersecting streams that teem with varmints. We're five miles south of Kingsville, Johnson County, Missouri (some fifty miles southeast of Kansas City), down in the second bottom of Big Creek. Log cabins nestle in the clearings with packed-dirt yards, a corncrib, root cellar, and spring house. This night in October 1869, a faint kerosene lamp glows from the store-bought window of the two-room log cabin occupied by Charles Burden and his family. The members are busy washing dishes after supper or shucking corn to make lye hominy.

Charles Burden stands (he is a strikingly handsome, tall, thin man with an athlete's physique) and says he's going to check the stock before turning in. He walks out the front door where Ol' Drum, a five-year-old black-and-tan hound, rises from sleep on the front porch and ambles close behind. They walk in the sodden leaves of a wet autumn; frost will sugar the land white by morning. Suddenly, Ol' Drum casts to the left and heads down into Big Creek. Immediately he strikes game, and the yip of his find pierces the air. The race is on. And Charles Burden stands to listen to the mellow bawls of his prized hound as the dog puzzles trail.

Later, Burden sits in a rocker on his front stoop, smoking home-spun tobacco in his corncob pipe. Suddenly, a gunshot claims the still night. Burden lurches forward, straining to listen. There is no other noise. But in his gut there's a wrenching hunch. He leaps to reach inside the doorway and grabs his hunting horn. He blows until all hounds appear at his feet but one—Ol' Drum. And somehow Burden knows. His brother-in-law, Leonidas "Lon" Hornsby, has killed his dog. For Hornsby has been losing sheep to wild dogs, and he has vowed he would kill the next one caught on his property.

Next morning Burden approaches Hornsby, who is pressing cider, and asks, "Lon, have you seen anything of Ol' Drum around here?" Lon replied he hadn't seen anything of him. Then came the question, "What about the dog you shot last night?" Hornsby said he hadn't shot any dog, but his hired hand, Dick, had. He added he thought the dog belonged to Davenport. Dick took Burden across the yard and showed him where he had shot the stray dog. Burden looked for traces of blood and found none. Then he returned to Hornsby and said, "I'll go hunt. It may not be my dog. If it ain't, it's all right. If it is, it's all wrong, and I'll have satisfaction at the cost of my life."

On the morning of October 29, Ol' Drum was found just a few feet above the ford in the creek below Haymaker's mill. He was dead, lying on his left side, with his head in the water, and his feet toward the dam, his body filled with shot of different sizes. Burden concluded Ol' Drum had been carried or dragged to this place: there was blood on his underside, his hair was bent backward, and there were sorrel hairs on his coat. Lon Hornsby owned a sorrel mule.

Burden headed for an attorney. Later he would tell another attorney (the case went to court four times), "When I found that Ol' Drum had been killed, I wanted to kill the man who did it. But I've seen too much of killings in the border warfare. And so I said, 'I'm going to go by law. I'm going to clear Ol' Drum's name. He was no sheep killer, and I'll prove to the world that Lon Hornsby killed him unrightfully if it's the last thing I do.'"

So came to pass the most noted dog trial in history on September 23, 1870. It concluded on a rainy night at the county courthouse in Warrensburg, Missouri, with the top legal talent of western Missouri arguing, what was by now, *the celebrated dog case*. One of the defendant's attorneys told the jury, "Such a lawsuit about a mere hound dog is of little value if not a neighborhood nuisance." But that didn't prove to be the case.

George Vest, principal attorney for Charles Burden, sat detached from the day-long proceedings. He was short, a bull of a man with thick neck, broad shoulders, fiery red hair, and a voice that would fire ice or melt steel as he would wish. All of Warrensburg turned out for the trial: it was like circus day. The restaurants were packed, the hitchracks taken, the livery stable filled. People who could not find accommodations intended to sleep in their rigs. And those who couldn't get into the courtroom peered in multiples through the courthouse windows, enduring a lightning storm and downpour. The sheriff had made sure no man entered the court with a gun. All inside sweltered in the high humidity. Only Vest never wiped his brow. As he was no part of these proceedings, neither was he part of the suffocation of the place.

For a moment let's examine the legal talent assembled for this hound's trial. Charles Burden had retained the partnership of Sedalia, Missouri's, John F. Phillips and George Graham Vest. The former would become a federal judge, the latter a United States senator.

Lon Hornsby countered with Thomas T. Crittenden, who later became governor of Missouri, and Francis Marion Cockrell, who ended up in the United States senate along with his adversary, George Vest. These were not mediocre men, nor had they met for a mediocre moment. Ol' Drum had pulled them all together for the most celebrated case in dogdom, as surely as he once rounded up every varmint that tried to take up residence on his beloved master's farm. And as these litigants made Ol' Drum immortal, the hound dog went a far way in making each of them a legend in his own time. None of them could eventually discount Ol' Drum's part in making their legal lives a success.

Now there was no court reporter for any of the four Ol' Drum trials. What is known about what happened there has come down to us from word of mouth. Men assembled later and reasoned together to put the court's testimony into writing. And this becomes important, as you will see.

George Vest stood. He rose scowling, mute, his eyes burning from under the slash of brow tangled as a grapevine. Then he stepped sideways, hooked his thumbs in his vest pockets, his gold watch fob hanging motionless. It was that heavy. And he said, "May it please the court," and began his oratory.

Gerald Carson, writing in *Natural History,* December 1969, relates: "Vest began to speak quietly and earnestly. He ignored the day's testimony. For about an hour he ranged through history, poetry, legend, and classical literature, calling attention to sagacious and faithful dogs whom men have loved, quoting from the Biblical account of the dogs who came to lick the sores of the beggar Lazarus; citing Byron's line in Don Juan, ' 'Tis sweet to hear the honest watchdog's bark'; and the graphic description in John Lathrop Motley's *The Rise of the Dutch*

Republic, of how a dog had prevented the capture of William of Orange by the cruel Duke of Alva.

"After pointing out the weaknesses in the arguments of opposing counsel and drawing attention to the law applicable to the case, Vest appeared ready to conclude. But then he moved closer to the jury box. He looked (someone remembered afterward) taller than his actual five feet six inches, and began in a quiet voice to deliver an extemporaneous oration. It was quite brief, less than four hundred words."

These are the immortal words Vest spoke:

"Gentlemen of the jury, the best friend a man has in the world may turn against him and become his worst enemy. His son or daughter that he has reared with loving care may prove ungrateful. Those who are nearest and dearest to us, those whom we trust with our happiness and our good name, may become traitors to their faith. The money that man has, he may lose. It flies away from him, perhaps when he needs it the most. A man's reputation may be sacrificed in a moment of ill-considered action. The people who are prone to fall on their knees to do us honor when success is with us may be the first to throw the stone of malice when failure settles its cloud upon our heads. The one absolutely unselfish friend that a man can have in this selfish world, the one that never deserts him and the one that never proves ungrateful or treacherous is his dog.

"Gentlemen of the jury, a man's dog stands by him in prosperity and in poverty, in health and in sickness. He will sleep on the cold ground, where the wintry winds blow and the snow drives fiercely, if only he may be near his master's side. He will kiss the hand that has no food to offer, he will lick the wounds and sores that come in encounters with the roughness of the world. He guards the sleep of his pauper master as if he were a prince. When all other friends desert he remains. When riches take wings and reputation falls to pieces, he is as constant in his love as the sun in its journey through the heavens. If fortune drives the master forth an outcast in the world, friendless and homeless, the faithful dog asks no higher privilege than that of accompanying him to guard against danger, to fight against his enemies, and when the last scene of all comes, and death takes the master in its embrace and his body is laid away in the cold ground, no matter if all other friends pursue their way, there by his graveside will the noble dog be found, his head between his paws, his eyes sad but open in alert watchfulness, faithful and true even to death."

The jury erupted in joint pathos and triumph. The record becomes sketchy here, but some say the plaintiff who was asking for $150 was awarded $500 by the jury. Little does that matter. The case was appealed to the Missouri Supreme Court, which refused to hear it.

What does matter is the eulogy to Ol' Drum has now been translated into most every language on earth and has been printed in excess of 200 million times.

Both litigants were bankrupted by the proceedings. They returned to their homes, living one mile apart, and time eventually healed their differences. At that place where Ol' Drum was found lying in the creek with the sorrel hairs embedded in his coat, a monument has been erected which once contained stones from every state in the union and practically every nation on earth. Before the new county courthouse in Warrensburg now stands a life-size bronze statue of Ol' Drum.

And if you journey five miles south of Kingsville, Johnson County, Missouri, tonight, you'll likely hear the plaintive call of some hound dog coursing the stream's woods, giving voice of his find, the night air ringing like an empty oil drum struck with a sledge at the music of his going.

There will always be an Ol' Drum. And a man to defend his honor.

Of Miracles
and Memories

I bought Wasatch Renegade and Uneva Drake's Lucky Lady when they were ten years old or more because they had once thrown two field champions out of the same litter. I was hoping these Labs could do it again. They never did, and it was many years later that Bob Wehle, of Midway, Alabama, the world's top gun-dog breeder, gave me insight into what happened. He told me he learned that producing males should be under a year old to throw great beget. He now knew, he said, the younger the better.

Well, anyway, I had many great gun dogs in their prime at that time, but on occasion I'd take Rene or Toughie, as the dam was called, to the duck blind.

It was a cold and iced-over late November dawn when Rene and I made the hunt. That afternoon I wrote what follows.

Old gun dogs have stood the test of time and event and circumstance. They come now, slowly, and lay at foot or close to side, jowls flat, eyes faded with the fog of cataract, their muzzles and paws white or speckled salt and pepper. But they come. They want to be close.

They are great treasures, these old dogs. Lying there, they are more than themselves. They are us. Parts of us. A hill climbed together and the crimson leaves of sumac danced in the morning sunlight. The well looked in and the rock dropped; the chill of the dark hole seemed to go on forever before the splash was heard.

They are sweaty palms, for you were hosting your boss and he'd never gunned over a trained dog before. But Pup was so birdy you couldn't be sure he'd hold for shot and wing.

They are the iced mace of wind thrown by bad-dad winter, off to the north, blowing the red-leg mallards off their winter haunts. Blowing them south, flying like buckshot. And you're gripping Pup and whispering, "No head up," as you fit the duck call to your lips. It is so cold you know it will freeze to the skin. But you call. And the lead hen throws her body high, looking down and back, seeing the iced-in blocks pointing bill-up to the slate sky.

And now they come, shingles ripped loose from some old barn. The wind is driving them crazily toward your decoys, and you stand and the old gun barks and the dog launches. He's breaking ice and standing high in the water, though his feet don't touch bottom. And you wish you'd never shot. For nothing can live out there—not even Pup in the prime of his life. Yet he clomps the big bright drake and spins about, throwing water with his whipping tail. He comes for you—the drake covering his face—swimming by instinct, for he cannot see.

You're out of the blind now and running the bank, yelling out. The retriever comes to shore, not stopping to shake, and heads straight for you. But the black dog turns instantly silver. The water has frozen that fast. You take the duck and the dog shivers, his teeth chattering, and the pelvic-drive muscles convulse. Then he spins in the tall yellow grass: he runs and rubs the side of his jowls in the mud and stubble.

No duck is worth this—remember saying that?—and the two of you go back to the house. Back to the towel you rub over Pup and the fire you sit before as the wind makes a harmonica of your house-siding and whomps down the fireplace to billow the ashes.

But the duck does lay on the sideboard by the sink. You entered nature, went duck hunting, tricked the wildfowl to your trap, and the dog closed the door.

Still, you're sorry you went; but years later, when the smell of that day's wet fur is forgotten and the curled tail feathers from the mallard have long been blown from the fireplace mantle, you'll remember that retrieve and old Pup will come to side. You'll fondle his ears and the memory of that cold day and that single duck will become the most important thing that ever happened in your life.

For Pup is dying.

You can't see him, but you have to smile and call him to you. It may be the last time you ever touch his ear. But that's just part of it. You're dying, too (we all are, you know). Pup just will go first. As he always went first in the field and at the blind. You followed him, not the other way around. It was he who entered the unknown and learned its bareness or its bounty.

You love the old dog, for he lived your life. He was the calendar of your joy. Why, you could leap the stream when you got your first pup. Remember? And you could hunt all day. Cold? Bosh! And the apple in your pocket was all it took to fuel you from Perkins's fence to Hadley's barn—a limit of bobwhite later.

But now the arthritis hobbles you. And the cold. It seems to come and sit in your bones like an unwanted stranger.

So you don't just call Pup to side, you call your life. You run your fingers through your past when you fondle his ears.

You stand and go to the gun case. Why, the bluing's gone from that old Superposed. Then you remember when you bought it: long before Pup ever came into your life. And look at that duck call. There's no varnish left on the barrel. And the barrel is cracked! And the string that holds it. It was a country store back in the hills; you stopped for hamburger to feed Pup. And the duck call was in your pocket, just out of its cardboard box. You asked the proprietor for a piece of string and he went to the meat counter and drew off a yard of it. You were always going to get a bona fide, braided lanyard.

But that's like life. You were always going to. . . .

And there's Pup. He was not a going to. He was a was. Not a put-off till tomorrow. Pup was planned and bought and trained and taken to field. That happened. And the million dollars was never made, and you never became branch manager, and your kids didn't make it through college. But Pup did all you imagined for him.

Pup was your one success.

And he is dying.

How many pups ago was it your sweater fitted loose on your belly, and your belly was hard like the barrel of a cannon? But look at the sweater now. Stretched tight and tattered and faded. Why do you still wear it? There are Christmas sweaters still in their boxes on the shelf in the closet.

And the boots. Remember? They had to be just so. But look at them now. Toes out, scuffed, heels run over. And yet you shuffle about in them.

Is it because you're holding on to the past? Is it because looking back down the road means more than looking on up ahead? Is it because the birds you went with Pup to get were got? And now? What do they say? A bird in the hand is worth more than two—maybe that's it. Pup made you a bird-in-the-hand man.

Others, in those days, may have been two-bird hopefuls. But you and Pup did it. You went. No sunshine patriots then. No sir. That bird was in hand.

He's got bad teeth now, you know? Pup has. And let's admit it: his breath stinks. And look at him, great blotches of hair hang here and there like some derelict mountain sheep that's taken to roadside begging. And he does little but sleep—and pass gas. He does lots of that.

There are pups to be bought, you know? Why, ads are everywhere.

And some say gun dogs have gotten better than ever. Or at least the training methods have gotten so sharp you can even bring a mediocre pup along.

But no. It's always been you and Pup. And you'll wait till he's no more. But have you ever wondered? What will you be when he's gone?

If he was the best part of your days, then what will there be when he's dead and buried? What will there be of you? Some grumpy old mumbler who sits by the fire and harrumphs at those who come to be kind?

No, not at all. For you were a gun-dog man and you went to field. Your Pup was the best gun dog you ever saw. And you watched the flash of the great black dog as he leaped through bramble and you saw him once atop the hill. How far away was he on that cast? A half mile! And all you must do is close your eyes; better yet, just go to the window and watch the falling leaves. Pup's out there. He's by the gate. See him? And he's leaping that way he always did, urging you to get on with it. And he darts now, to the field, and sniffs the passing mice, the dickey birds.

And then you're with him, the weight of the gun reassuring in your grasp. Your stride is strong and the wind bites your cheek, but you laugh and blow the white steam of cold. Always you can do this, just standing at the window—for you did this.

What of the smell of straw at the old duck blind and pouring the coffee from the Thermos. Then learning how to pour the coffee from the steel cup so you could put the cup to your lips. And you never knew why the pouring made the cup manageable.

And the pride in your homemade decoys, watching them run to the end of their cords and spin about, ducking their heads and bobbing to drip water from their bills.

And off to the left, in that stand of multiflora rose: Hear him! The cock pheasant *car-runks*. Bright as brass he is. And you could heel Pup out of the duck blind and go get him, but you like his sass. You like his arrogance. And the fact that anything that gaudy can live out there in the back of your place.

And what of the morning you and Pup were sitting there? Duck hunting for you didn't mean shooting ducks. It meant being there. Hearing the rustle of your heavy canvas pants and the tinkle of the dog whistles and calls as they danced on your chest. Blowing in cupped hands, beating them against the sides of your chest. And standing and stomping on the wood pallets you brought in because the water rose with the late rains. And for that moment you and Pup were silent and the redtailed hawk landed, right above both of you, on a naked limb.

You were ornery. Jumped up, you did, and yelled, "Hey, Hawk!" And the hawk was so discombobulated he hurled himself to the air with a great squawk, leaving a white stream all over your blind as he beat his departure. But it was still funny, and you sat in the draping of hawk feces—and laughed.

Not another single living thing had that moment but you and Pup and the hawk. And the three of you made that moment momentous forever. The hawk is gone and Pup is going but that moment makes you all vibrant and alive. And in a way it makes you important. Who else ever had an exclusive moment?

And if Pup had not taken you to field, you'd not have had it. So he lays there now, that generator of meaning and memory. That's what a gun dog comes to be for us. An enricher of life. Something to take ordinary moments and make them miraculous.

That's why the love for Pup is so great. What matter if he passes gas and has bad breath and moans in his sleep. He's earned his transgressions. And he tells us of our own end. For sharing the best with him, we must now share the worst with him, and we lie there, too.

But dog men push that away. Their Pup was a springer spaniel, you know. Oh, how happy he was afield. Why, the stub of his tail couldn't be tallied as it wagged. And it wagged that way when idle or working. He was just that happy. And he made the man happy. For happiness is infectious, and there's no known cure. Not even disaster. For you'll walk around the knowledge of disaster to peek in memory at that happy tail.

And that man's Pup was a beagle. A mellow-voiced ground snorter if ever there was one. The bow legs, all that massed muscle. And how he used to launch the rabbit and then dart out in pursuit, giving the man instructions—Loud Instructions!—on when to shoot.

But that's not the Pup I was thinking of. No. That Pup was your cocker with thick hair the color of wheat tassels; he'd rut to launch the bird, down in the mud, going under the high-water log. And up he'd come with that smashed face, little mud balls hanging from his silver whiskers, and in a turn—which was more like a complete flip—he'd tell you with his body signal there was nothing down there and you'd best be off.

But who am I to talk like this? You know your Pup better than I ever could. For there was just the two of you—oh, maybe a hawk! And what happened can never happen again. No man and dog could ever be that rich, that lucky, that blessed again.

Yet, each year several million new pups are taken into American homes, into American hearts. All on the knowledge that there are some miracles and memories left out there yet.

JOE ARNETTE

Welcome to Hard Times

JOE ARNETTE is a former wild-life biologist who now devotes almost all of his time to dog training, hunting, and writing. He lives with his wife, Kathy, in Kennebunkport, Maine. In addition, there are two field-bred springer spaniels that live in the Arnette household.

He contributes regular columns to *Gun Dog, North American Hunter,* and the *Ruffed Grouse Society* magazines. Recently he has added a new assignment and become the Associate Editor for Countrysport Press.

Permission to use the story, "Welcome to Hard Times," in the anthology was given by the author.

He was a first-generation American, a springer spaniel of transplanted English parentage. From birth, he was destined to become a free-wheeling good ol' boy—full of hell, with more than his share of screws loose, lacking the slightest suggestion of a stiff-lipped lord of the British manor.

Yes, he was born in the USA. And together we had the days of seven seasons—not always great days, not always even acceptable days, but ever-interesting and occasionally monumental days.

Then he died here, much too soon, at not quite eight years old. At first, I thought that was why I ranked him so high on my personal short list of very good dogs; there hadn't been time to gain the wisdom of distance. Now, after enough years of separation, I know that wasn't the case.

He was wired motion—"supersonic," a friend tagged him—red hot and exceptionally athletic from the first. He ran with unmitigated flash, encumbered only by passion every step of his life, his liver-and-white body flowing like mercury behind a nose long with grouse and woodcock. This springer was indeed a damn Yankee, spontaneous and lacking the merest hint of moderation, born with a need to take life's corners on two wheels. He was a finished dog with a lilt in his gait and a let's-get-to-it attitude in his brain; a high-powered working stiff who showed up ready for every job and rarely failed to complete any of them. Until near the end. Then it was beyond him.

Toward the last days of what was to be his final bird season, the dog began to slow down. The change was almost imperceptible at first, no more than a mild tempering of his speed and his ability to bust brush. It wasn't a matter of willingness; his drive and push were there, but his body was showing signs of being elsewhere. When you live with a dog for seven years, you note such subtle shifts, especially in a springer who overrode pain and injury as a matter of course.

This was a dog who had hunted with a two-inch locust spine jammed to the hilt in the bones of his foot. He neither stopped to pull it out nor made a whimper over what must have been serious pain. When it became too much for him, he simply went up on three legs and continued to work until I whistled him to a stop and found the spine. This was a too-gritty dog that once hunted all morning, without a hitch in his step, on a pad gashed so badly that it later kept him off his feet for three weeks. I didn't find the cut until a normal, post-hunt exam, and from the damage it was clear that he had been running on it for hours. When such a single-minded dog tries to go but can't, however slight the signals, you look beyond the obvious.

Joe Arnette

I knew that something was wrong when he began walking in the final five to ten yards of his retrieves. After all, this was "supersonic," a spaniel who never walked; who would sit at a bird's flush and fall, leaning into it; and who, at his name, would rocket to the mark, pick it up in a pivoting cloud of dust, and be back in front of me before I could process what had just taken place. Walk on a retrieve?

Then, within a short period of time, he began to have a bit of trouble going up inclines. The first time his hindquarters caved in, on level ground, I had him in my veterinarian's office within a half-hour. His hips were perfect; besides, his troubles had developed too quickly and out of context for dysplasia. I assumed that his was a lower spinal problem, not entirely uncommon in fine-boned, superactive dogs.

Anal-gland cancer and its associated immediacy of mortality never occurred to me.

My vet, a friend, gave me an honest appraisal of the dog's condition and a straightforward look at my options—or, rather, my springer's options. None of them even approached being acceptable. This was a raging form of cancer that had leapfrogged from nothing to something to everything in a few months.

Discussions with veterinary oncologists pointed out just one thing and pointed it out quite clearly: Their ideas of successful treatment and mine were more than worlds apart. Surgery was their job; to me and my dog it was personal. Full-scale treatment to gain perhaps an unpleasant month or two was something that had to be weighed against the unquestioned inevitable. Only the timing, not the end, was in doubt. My decision was both easy and difficult. This dog was born with élan and lived to run and hunt. I would not allow him to die as a pain-ridden shadow unable to rise from his bed.

The details of the last days are unimportant. Suffice it to say that they revolved around comfort and catering and a sense of the moment. I think, now, that I may have allowed that time to go on too long, but right and wrong, appropriate and inappropriate, can become hazy concepts that lack form and clear definition. Reality is a judgment of the moment.

Woodcock were back in the spring coverts in numbers when that judgment came. Legality and penalties had no place in my thoughts when I entered a favored piece of cover and shot the first bird I found. My idea of the right thing to do had lifted me to a higher, or at least more immediate, moral level. Woodcock and I had been the two primary forces in this springer's life, and I intended him to have both close by his side as he left his seasons behind.

I drove back with the dog to that favorite covert—the one that he had hunted so well, so many times—and parked on an old logging road that led to its interior. We sat, or rather I sat while he curled next to me, on the truck's tailgate, where we had spent the time of seven years before and after hunts. The woodcock lay between his paws. He put his head on it and stared into the covert. Anything else was beyond his strength.

The sedative I gave him worked rapidly, and he was deeply asleep when we arrived at the vet's. My friend came out and did what was necessary as the spaniel slept in the truck with his head still on the woodcock and with my hand resting gently along the creamy curve of his neck.

Welcome to hard times.

The stiff wind rolling off the river blew this springer spaniel's ashes, blended inseparably with those of the last woodcock of his short life, through the alders and into the abutting pines. The gray-white cloud did not linger in the breeze, though it hung for a moment against the dark of the conifers. Then it took off and was gone.

I think that my hard-going springer would have appreciated the quickness of his ashes' departure. During his seasons as a freewheeling gun dog, he hadn't been one to linger when it was time to go.

CLIFF SCHROEDER

Smokey

CLIFF SCHROEDER wrote this moving piece about the relationship between the bird dog and its master for the May/June 1983 issue of *Gun Dog* magazine. From the extraordinarily descriptive writing in "Smokey," you know that Mr. Schroeder has been there.

We made an extensive search to locate Cliff Schroeder. With the change in ownership of *Gun Dog* magazine, the editorial office records for the early issues did not have addresses for many of the authors. Thus, we were not successful in contacting Mr. Schroeder. However, we thought his story was one that should be included in our celebration of bird dogs. We hope that he would think so, too.

The first crisp October morning stirred deep memories in the old dog even before he was awake. Lying on the rug by the door, his feet twitched and saliva formed at the corners of his mouth as visions of past Octobers touched his mind. He whimpered softly as he dreamed he caught the smell of grouse, of spent shells, and of frosty aspen woods.

Then they stirred in the house, and he came awake slowly, lifting his square old head from its cradle between his paws. Before he was fully awake, he saw Him standing in the doorway with His old hunting coat on and the broken double tucked under His arm. Then he knew it wasn't Him because he had heard no footsteps, and there was no gentle hand on his head. It had been so long now that even the odors of Him had faded from the house. Lately, he could find it only by the hallway closet upstairs or, on damp days, by the workbench at the front of the garage. And they wondered why on rainy days he liked to curl up on the wood shavings and dust that had collected under the workbench.

Lately, the boy opened the door for him, and slowly, because of the aching in his legs, he pulled himself up with proper dignity and stepped out. The grass was wet with dew, and across the near pasture, small eddies of mist were rising in the early sun. He circled the yard slowly, stopping now and then to sniff out some scent, but his mind was on other things. Once some woodcock winged overhead, and he stopped for a long time looking off into the direction they had gone.

When he came to the turn-off, where a two-track trail followed the rail fence before it dipped into the oak and maple grove, he paused again. He turned his head to look at the house where smoke rose from the chimney and from which came the tantalizing odor of bacon and coffee. There were some clattering noises from the house, and soon they would come out to the garage and leave in the car. He sat down and waited.

Over by the pines, some crows were calling. The old dog heard them, but they were not important to him. The sun was coming through now, and he turned just slightly to get its warmth on his back. After a few minutes, he lay down and stretched out, his head toward the house, his eyes shut.

He heard the garage door open and, standing, watched them drive away. Now there was no hesitation. He turned down the trail toward the grove of trees and began to trot. Once he got going and some of the stiffness was gone, he felt pretty good. He pranced just a little and carried his feathered tail at a confident angle. His feet left slight pad marks in the sandy dust of the trail.

When he entered the grove, he surprised a blue jay that had been on the ground looking for acorns. The jay flew up in the tree and voiced his outrage. The old dog turned his head as he trotted by and grinned.

Beyond the grove was the rolling pasture—down a hollow and up along a gentle ridge. Grasshoppers were warming up in the sun and whirred across the trail as he came by. Occasionally, the old dog turned and looked back down the trail, but there was no one there.

At the edge of the pasture, the trail entered the nearby woods and became a narrow log-skidding trail. This was as far as the dog had ever gone by himself. He'd always had the run of the pasture where, since puppy days, he had chased butterflies and played games with swooping barn swallows. The pasture was close enough for a whistle to bring him back for the meal or for the Jeep ride to town. Beyond the pasture was the hunting country, and they had always shared that.

So, at the edge of the woods, the old dog turned and studied his back trail. When that did not satisfy him, he stepped off the trail and trotted up a slight rise. From this vantage, he could see most of the trail he had come and, barely through the trees, some white of the house showed through.

Suddenly, it all seemed very familiar. This was where he had always waited for Him. After rushing excitedly ahead, here he would wait for Him so they could enter the woods together. At any moment now, the well-known form would emerge from the grove of trees and come toward him up the trail.

Now the dog made a show of waiting, impatiently jumping up on his back feet and sounding sharp, short barks of excitement. He paced back and forth between the approaching trail and the woods and almost expected to hear a mild, amused voice chiding him for his impatience. But there was no voice, and the dog turned to face the trail and stood quietly.

There was no casual, half-slouching figure coming up the trail, no cheerful whistle, no blue eyes looking directly into his liquid brown eyes. The dog stood statue-like with the breeze coming across the pasture softly rippling his feathered legs and tail. There was an almost, but not quite, imperceptible sag to his shoulders and head.

Suddenly, the dog turned and trotted briskly up the trail into the woods. He must be up ahead somewhere, waiting by some alder thicket or resting on a convenient stump.

The old dog was headed for the far woods. The trail he was on ran through these woods for perhaps a quarter mile, winding between aspen trees broken by patches of spruce or balsam, then across a series of low-lying meadows, and into the larger forest known as the far woods. The dog quickened his pace. He paid scant heed to the chickadees that flitted from tree to tree ahead of him, uttering their cheerful chatter. Once he was brought up short by the throaty twang of a nuthatch, but the illusion that it was a voice he knew was only momentary.

At the edge of the meadow, he startled two deer that bounded off, tails high, until they realized the old dog was no threat to them. When the dog hurried on with only a sideways glance, the curious deer stopped and came back a few hesitant steps, noses outstretched and tails half-raised.

The dog continued his pace, sometimes turning his head to the side, but not wavering from the trail that was becoming more over-grown. Some of the tall grasses leaned over the path, and the dog's shoulders brushed dew from their tasseled tops.

Ahead, the trail tunneled into the darker forest. These were large, mature trees, white pine with scraggly tops in the sky, wide northern red oak on the high ground, and clumps of black-trunked basswoods on the edges of low land. Here were large male aspen with their buds that fed the grouse in winter. Here were thick spruce that protected the grouse from winds in the wet, cold autumn days, and held the snow in deep drifts for their survival in sub-zero winter nights. This

was prime grouse country, a grouse hunter's—and a grouse dog's—heaven.

Now the old dog's purposefulness was gone. He seemed to alternate between random wanderings down faded old cross trails and standing for long, pensive moments at some turn in the trail. Once he nosed among the leaves near a wide stump and finally uncovered the old wax-paper wrappings of a sandwich. He waited near the stump for longer than usual, sitting quietly with alert eyes and moist nose.

Wandering on, the dog showed near-excitement at several places. In an alder thicket at the edge of a grassy marsh, he circled and re-circled with his graceful tail waving slowly. When he paused, his eyes looked off through the trees into the distance.

Vaguely, the dog realized that he was in the presence of his happiest memories. Here he had spent the Octobers of his life. As a young pup with awkward, gangly legs and a speckled face, he had pointed his first grouse for Him. And he had learned the purpose of life—to scent the woods-birds with thunder in their wings, point them for Him, and retrieve the downed bird for His warm praise and for the touch of His hand on his head.

Smokey

So they had grown old together doing the things they loved together. The essence of life was condensed for them into a bright autumn day, a walk in the woods, a thunder of wings, the smell of gunpowder, and a shared sandwich from the pocket of an old hunting coat.

Quietly, the old dog stepped through the golden, autumnal woods. His pace was slowed, and he seemed confused as he looked vaguely about him. Several times he stumbled, rustling the bright leaves that he walked on.

Suddenly, like the clear sound of a note, like a stream of cold water, it came to him—the most delectable scent of his world. Slowly, so slowly, he turned his head, his nose bringing him the direction of the grouse. One front foot was up and it did not move. He leaned slightly forward, back legs wide and feathered tail raised.

And there they were—the birds! Two of them behind a small clump of brush. They eyed each other, the birds and the dog. And He was there too. The old dog could feel His presence just back of him, so he waited.

Saliva drooled from the corners of his mouth. He rolled his eyes back to see if He was coming in or waiting. He knew he could hold this point forever, but a heaviness and drowsiness seemed to be pulling him down. With a deep sigh, the old dog sank to the ground, tail laid straight out and head resting on the ground, but still pointed at the watchful birds.

For one long moment, there was a hush in the forest, no bird sounds, no wind in the trees, no rustling of leaves. There was only the sunlight shafting through the trees to light up the bright October leaves, and the white, black, and golden form that lay on them. A large basswood leaf, veined and brown as a man's hand, fell from the tree above. It drifted slowly down, twirling and spinning, till it settled lightly on the old dog's head. The old dog closed his eyes as he felt again the gentlest touch he had ever known.

TOM S. COOPER

A Gift Beyond Measure

TOM COOPER wrote this article, entitled "A Gift Beyond Measure," which was published in *Field & Stream* magazine in January 2001. We wrote to Tom Cooper in March of 2001 and received permission to use his piece in this anthology. However, two years later when we were preparing the authors' biographies and contacting them for information, we were unable to locate Tom Cooper. We made an extensive telephone search in an effort to find him in the Clarksdale, Mississippi, area; unfortunately, we were not successful.

The pair of Llewellin setters were barking like crazy, eager to get out of the metal dog trailer attached to my old Jeep. When I opened the door, the younger dog, Tex, bounded out first. The older setter, Buck, was less agile; his slight arthritic limp was the painful result of eight tough seasons of hunting.

Both wore bells so I could locate them easily in the dense thickets and tall sedge that quail call home. In addition, Tex dragged a 10-foot section of yellow ski rope. The rope helped slow him down, and it also allowed me to grab hold of him when he chose not to honor Buck's points. As the dogs dashed away, my partner, Jerry, and I basked in the Mississippi winter day. Overcast skies, temperature in the low 40s, and a nippy breeze from the north—perfect quail weather.

A Gift Beyond Measure

I watched Buck race to a nearby thicket. I couldn't help but feel a sense of pride. He was a crackerjack bird dog, always hunting boldly and with enthusiasm. He would venture into birdy places fearlessly, frequently coming back scratched and bloodied. His limp was a sign that he had already seen his best hunting days. It would surely be only a short time before he would have to hand over the reins to his bracemate, Tex.

Tex was a youngster, not yet two years old. He showed lots of promise, but he ran with such abandon that one bird hunter had astutely described him as "having legs that were faster than his nose."

Buck seemed to know intuitively that he had to get to the birds before the young pup found them. As a result, I noticed that the older dog tended to run farther out each time we hunted.

The dogs soon disappeared into a big drainage ditch so thick with briers and honeysuckle that I figured we would have no chance to get a shot, so I whistled the dogs back. Neither responded. Reluctantly I entered the ditch. As I fought through the brambles, a covey of quail flushed. The sound of the rise startled me, but my pump reflexively went to my shoulder and I got off a wild shot. I didn't see a bird fall, so I continued fighting through the jungle.

I maneuvered down into the creek bed and with difficulty climbed up the other bank, blowing my whistle frequently. I heard the tinkling of Buck's bell coming from a 10-year-old stand of pine trees. He obviously was in the area where the singles had gone, but knowing it would be fruitless to hunt this dense thicket, I kept calling the dogs back. Tex finally returned; Buck was nowhere to be seen.

Jerry and I began to hunt the field edges and hedgerows with Tex. As we walked along, I was embarrassed that my prized dog was performing poorly in front of my comrade. I said, "Jerry, I haven't whipped a dog in years, but Buck and I are going to come to an understanding."

I went over to a nearby thicket and cut a small sapling with my pocketknife.

The pup entered a strip of bicolor lespedeza 20 yards ahead of us. He held his tail erect as he tiptoed stylishly through the head-high brush. But then a bobwhite hen came roaring out the other side; Tex had carelessly flushed up a single that flew out of range of our guns.

I was really steaming when I finally heard the soft clang of Buck's bell. He was hobbling through the sedge toward me. I was preparing to tan his hide when I noticed that he held a bobwhite gingerly in his mouth. My jaw dropped wide open, and the switch fell to the ground. I went to my knees, took the tired old dog's head in my hands, and hugged him. I felt about 6 inches tall.

🌿 🌿 🌿

The following summer, the veterinarian told me that Buck's arthritis was actually bone cancer. There was nothing he could do except make Buck as comfortable as possible until the end.

After Buck died I buried him in the same field where he had brought me that bird. As I laid him to rest I thought about that day when an old dog gave me a gift beyond measure—a lesson in humility, loyalty, and spirit.

DR. TOM HOLCOMB, DVM

What Would You Do If I Was Your Dog, Doc?

DR. TOM HOLCOMB is a practicing Doctor of Veterinary Medicine (DVM) in Adel, Iowa. He received his DVM from Iowa State University in Ames, Iowa, in 1965. He and his wife, Mary Lea, have two children, a son and daughter, and four grandchildren. His son is also a practicing veterinarian.

Dr. Holcomb has been writing a column called "The Veterinary Clinic" for *Gun Dog* magazine since the first issue was published in September/October of 1981. This feature has provided expert medical advice to gun-dog owners for over twenty years. The magazine is published six times a year, so through the year 2002, Dr. Tom has written 126 columns. He has not missed a single issue.

Euthanasia, mercy killing, "putting to sleep," "putting down" are all words or phrases used to denote what Mr. Webster defined as "the act or practice of killing or permitting the death of hopelessly sick or injured individuals (as persons or domestic animals) in a relatively painless way for reasons of mercy." Obviously, we can't encompass in a definition such as this all the emotion, fear, anger, depression, and denial that are involved in arriving at and carrying out the decision to have a dog euthanized.

Dr. Tom Holcomb, DVM

In addition, he has on several occasions written a specific piece for *Gun Dog*. With his permission, "What Would You Do If I Was Your Dog, Doc?" is included in this collection. It originally appeared in the September/October 1985 issue of *Gun Dog* magazine.

The two common situations that I find clients dealing with are the older dog with a terminal illness and the dog that is severely injured, usually from a car accident. The old dog, suffering from chronic kidney disease, liver problems, cancer, or whatever, deserves certain considerations before the decision is made to put a longtime friend to sleep.

First of all, these individuals should be given an adequate chance to recover. I'm continually amazed at the recuperative powers of some of these old troopers. Secondly, use these guidelines in assessing whether an animal's life is being prolonged with unnecessary unpleasantness: Does the dog have any tumors that cause pain or serious discomfort and cannot be removed surgically? Can the dog pass urine and have bowel movements without pain or serious difficulty or incontinence? As the owner, are you able to cope with the nursing care this dog requires? Does the dog breathe without difficulty? Does it eat and drink enough to maintain itself and without vomiting? And, most importantly, is the dog living relatively free of pain, distress, or serious discomfort which cannot be controlled?

Age is an important consideration when involved surgeries or long complex medical regimens are anticipated, especially when there is little hope of extending the dog's life to any significant degree. This has come to the forefront in human medicine, as well, in recent years, with the advent of the "living will." Other weights to use in this balance of life and death are the emotional relationship or attachment to this animal and, by all means, the feelings of the other family members toward the dog. I tell my clients that time should be taken for a family meeting with open discussion of the dog's situation and possible paths for a resolution.

What Would You Do If I Was Your Dog, Doc?

Finally and unfortunately, money may be a deciding factor for some families. As a young graduate with my altruistic scalpel and syringe in hand, I had the view that all animals should be infinitely cared for, but, as I grow older and raise my own family, I can understand the reluctance to spend large sums when family finances are tight. People are still more important than dogs.

Once the decision is made to have a dog euthanized, a series of events begins, often proceeding rapidly and in a confusing manner, especially when punctuated with extreme emotion. Things like: what method to use; who will sign the release form; is it your desire to be present when the act is performed; and what to do about the dog's body. These all fly by so rapidly, decisions may be made in haste and without regard for logical reasoning. A first consideration should be the method of euthanasia. This will probably be a personal choice of your veterinarian, but you should assure yourself that it is a humane procedure. Two drugs are currently used and seem to be free of suffering. These are sodium pentobarbital which is a general anesthetic and is simply given as an overdose, and the dog goes quietly "to sleep" and on to death; and a new drug called T-61 which is a combination of a general anesthetic, muscle relaxant, and local anesthetic, and acts similarly to pentobarb but a little faster. Other drugs and techniques have been advocated in the past but are now in disfavor due to inhumane aspects. These include electrocution, CO_2 chambers, decompression, and the drug, succinylcholine chloride—avoid these at all costs.

Most veterinarians now ask that owners sign a standard euthanasia release form. This is used to release the veterinarian from any liability for destroying the animal and to verify that the dog could not have bitten anyone recently or been exposed to rabies. It most assuredly does not give anyone permission to use the dog for research purposes either before or after death.

I always give clients the option of being with their pet when I perform the euthanasia. In our clinic, over half of the people want to be present. I'm not sure what psychological significance to attach to this, but it does point out the commitment and responsibility we have when we undertake animal ownership. It is a privilege to own animals—not a right—and, as such, we are entrusted with their lives and deaths.

Currently, the human-animal bond is receiving much play in both the scientific and popular press. The area of pet death/owner grief has been explored and those stages of grief that people go through with human deaths are the same grieving processes that they go through over their pets. We must approach the grieving pet owner with care and not respond inappropriately to things that might seem silly or bizarre to us. I've noticed some breed publications are printing obituaries and memorials to dogs. I like that. They may be buried in our hearts but they're still remembered in our stories.

From a veterinarian's view, euthanasia is the most difficult thing we do. Some days I try to approach it with a very analytical, rational attitude; at other times, I find myself as emotionally involved as the owners. It is difficult to kill old friends you have cared for for twelve, fourteen, or more years. It is difficult to tell a fifteen-year-old child that his fifteen-year-old dog is at the end of the road of life. We must consider the emotions of all involved when an animal is euthanized.

I knew a boy in eighth grade whose dog was causing trouble in the neighborhood. One day it was gone, with the explanation that a farm home had been found for "Tip." On a Sunday afternoon, two or three weeks later, the boy's fingers began to tremble, his arm contracted, and he collapsed to the floor. Fortunately, he was attended by a good family doctor who immediately diagnosed the problem and prescribed the cure. When the boy awoke, a little brown-and-white rat terrier pup was licking him on the face. I named her "Pill."

CHARLES W. GUSEWELLE

Archaeology

CHARLES W. GUSEWELLE graduated in 1955 from Westminster College and joined *The Kansas City Star* that year as a general assignment reporter. He became an editorial writer on foreign affairs in 1966 and foreign editor in 1976. He resides with his wife, Katie, in the Kansas City area.

Besides his newspaper reporting and commentary, his articles and short fiction have appeared in *Harper's, American Heritage, The Paris Review,* and many other magazines and journals. He was awarded *The Paris Review's* Aga Khan Prize for Fiction in 1977. He was the subject in 1979 of a 30-minute film produced under sponsorship of the National Endowment for the Humanities. The film was one in a series of three on Midwestern writers.

He has authored six books

In some future year, a different proprietor of the land, out walking on a fine spring day, may pass that way—along the abandoned fencerow where the blackberry canes are white with bloom and the wild rose makes mounds of pink at the field's edge. That brushy line, in which no posts or wire remain, divides two meadows of native grass that fall away toward the dark of woods on either side.

The walker will discover, tucked in close against a thicket, a curious mound of flat fieldstones, too neatly placed and fitted to be accidental. Curiosity will bring him back there another day, carrying a shovel.

including the most recent in 1996, *The Rufus Chronicle: Another Autumn*, which is currently available as a Ballantine Book.

For nearly thirteen years, from earliest puppyhood, the bird dog Rufus was a recurring character in Charles W. Gusewelle's thrice-weekly column in the newspaper. Through Rufus, Gusewelle celebrated the Brittany, recording his escapades, misdemeanors, and triumphs.

The following short piece, entitled "Archaeology," was originally published in the book, *The Rufus Chronicle: Another Autumn*. The author has given permission for the piece to be used in this collection.

He will lift the stones aside and excavate beneath them, possibly imagining a treasure. But what he will unearth will be only the folded skeleton of a dog, and four large plastic buttons of the kind found on a canvas hunting coat. Also, if he looks carefully, the wing bones—finer than matchsticks—of a small bird.

If that man is a hunter, he will understand immediately what he's found. He will know that the creatures those artifacts represent are gone from there, away to some field of always autumn. I like to think he will replace the earth and stones, and leave the place as it was—a little cache of things that tell no story except when all together—safe again from rushing time.

Where to Bury a Dog

BEN HUR LAMPMAN was born in Wisconsin before the turn of the century on August 12, 1886. His formal schooling was cut short when he ran away from home at the age of fifteen, eventually to become a journalist who edited a small newspaper in North Dakota. He married a vibrant young schoolteacher from New York and they moved west to settle on the banks of the Rogue River in Oregon, where he enjoyed a career as a fisherman-printer-writer. Later he became an associate editor of the *Portland Oregonian,* in which he wrote the piece, "Where to Bury a Dog."

Lampman received a Master of Arts degree in 1943 from the University of Oregon, and an honorary Doctor of Laws from the University of Portland in

A subscriber of the *Ontario Argus* has written to the editor asking, "Where shall I bury my dog?" It is asked in advance of death.

We would say to the Ontario man that there are various places in which a dog may be buried. We are thinking now of a setter, whose coat was flame in the sunshine, and who, so far as we are aware, never entertained a mean or an unworthy thought. This setter is buried beneath a cherry tree, under four feet of garden loam, and at its proper season the cherry strews petals on the green lawn of his grave. Beneath a cherry tree, or an

Ben Hur Lampman

1947. He was named Oregon's first Poet Laureate in 1951, and received the O. Henry Memorial Award. His editorial writings, essays, and poems were published in several books, including a volume on fishing entitled *A Leaf from French Eddy,* published posthumously in 1965.

Ben Hur Lampman had an Irish setter, which was apparently not used to pursuing upland birds. The setter was a companion, and Lampman grieved the loss of this beloved pet.

We appreciate and acknowledge the permission granted by Ms. Monica Sullivan and Amwell Press for the use of Ben Hur Lampman's story, entitled "Where to Bury a Dog." This story and the above biography appeared in the anthology, *The Bird Dog Book,* edited by George Bird Evans and published by Amwell Press in 1979.

apple, or any flowering shrub of the garden, is an excellent place to bury a good dog. Beneath such trees, such shrubs, he slept in the drowsy summer, or gnawed at a flavorous bone, or lifted head to challenge some strange intruder. These are good places, in life or in death. Yet it is a small matter. For if the dog be well remembered, if sometimes he leaps through your dreams actual as in life, eyes kindling, laughing, begging, it matters not at all where that dog sleeps. On a hill where the wind is unrebuked, and the trees are roaring, or beside a stream he knew in puppyhood, or somewhere in the flatness of a pasture land, where most exhilarating cattle graze. It is all one to the dog, and all one to you, and nothing is gained, and nothing lost—if memory lives. But there is one best place to bury a dog.

If you bury him in this spot, he will come to you when you call—come to you over the grim, dim frontiers of death, and down the well-remembered path, and to your side again. And though you call a dozen living dogs to heel they shall not growl at him, nor resent his coming, for he belongs there. People may scoff at you, who see no lightest blade of grass bent by his footfall, who hear no whimper, people who may never really have had a dog. Smile at them, for you shall know something that is hidden from them, and which is well worth the knowing. The one best place to bury a good dog is in the heart of his master.

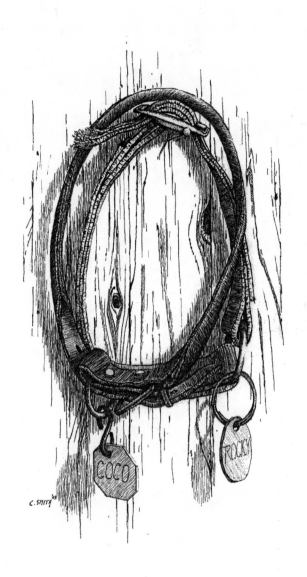

LaVergne, TN USA
27 November 2009
165413LV00002B/3/P